DEVOTIONS FOR ADVENTUROUS BOYS

MATT KOCEICH

DEVOTIONS FOR ADVENTUROUS BOYS

180 DAYS OF BRAVE-HEARTED ENCOURAGEMENT

BARBOUR **kidz**

A Division of Barbour Publishing

Published by Barbour Publishing, Inc., 1810 Barbour Drive, Uhrichsville, Ohio 44683, www.barbourbooks.com

Our mission is to inspire the world with the life-changing message of the Bible.

Member of the Evangelical Christian Publishers Association

Printed in China.

002164 0924 DS

BRAVE

/brāv/
adjective

1. SHOWING COURAGE.

You are very, very special!

God has created you to do great things for Him and His glory. The cool part is that He doesn't wait for you to become a grown-up. Right now, God wants to grow you into an adventurous, brave boy so you can become a young man of integrity—that is, a young man who lives by God's principles.

Remember the story of David and Goliath? That's a great example of how God used a young person to do a job that even soldiers were afraid to do.

The giant was scary and mean. The word in Hebrew that describes him is *ish habbenayim*, or *champion*. The word literally translates "the man of the two spaces." A river divided the valley where the Israelites and Philistine troops were positioned. The giant was so big and intimidating that people saw him as being in charge of *both spaces*.

That's what fear does to people. It makes them forget how big God really is.

But a champion who bullied God's people was really no winner at all.

David saw what was happening and knew something had to be done. You know how the story ends. David took out the mighty man with just one stone from his slingshot.

It's time for you to be encouraged and discover the great plans God has for your life.

YOU ARE ADVENTUROUS AND BRAVE!

GOD'S GOT THIS!

*"The Lord your God is the One Who goes
with you. He will be faithful to you."*
DEUTERONOMY 31:6

One of the very first lessons we learn about being brave comes from the garden of Eden. You may be familiar with the story, but let's look at Adam and Eve and see how things went for them. God had planted a beautiful garden for His first people to enjoy. He told the first couple to enjoy everything He had created for them, except they were to stay away from a particular tree.

Sometime later the devil showed up and went right to Eve with a question. This is where Adam had a chance to be brave but failed miserably! The devil tempted Eve to do what she wanted instead of obeying what God had said. Adam, if he had been brave, would have stuck up for God and refused to listen to the devil's lies. But he didn't, and sin entered the world.

Being brave means doing things God's way!

GOD, I KNOW THAT YOU ARE ALL-POWERFUL. PLEASE HELP ME TO BECOME THE BRAVE BOY YOU WANT ME TO BE. I PRAY THAT I WON'T BE DRAWN TO THINGS THAT WILL KEEP ME FROM FOLLOWING YOU. I PRAY THAT LOVING YOU IS ALWAYS MY TOP PRIORITY. BY YOUR SPIRIT, I WANT TO KNOW ALL THE THINGS YOU FEEL ABOUT ME.

BE HONEST

"Do not be afraid or troubled.
Be strong and have strength of heart."
JOSHUA 10:25

Another important part in letting God mold you into a brave boy is being honest with God. After Adam and Eve disobeyed God, they hid in the garden, ashamed for what they'd done. God called to Adam, "Where are you?" Can you imagine? The God of the universe personally calls your name! But that's exactly what God is doing today. He's calling you to live a brave life for His glory.

Adam could have tried to stay hidden or even lied, but he knew that God was reaching out to him. He quickly confessed to eating the fruit of the forbidden tree. Becoming brave God's way means going to Him and telling Him your mistakes. Talk to God daily. Through His Word, let Him teach you the right way to act. The devil wants you to feel afraid and scared after you make a mistake. He wants you to feel bad.

Pray to be brave!

LORD, EVEN THOUGH A LOT OF CRAZY THINGS HAPPEN IN THE WORLD AROUND ME, I LOOK FORWARD TO THE CHALLENGE OF BEING A BRAVE BOY. THANK YOU FOR GIVING ME YOUR HOLY SPIRIT TO LIVE INSIDE ME AND MAKE ME STRONG. HELP ME TO STAY GROUNDED IN YOUR TRUTH. I LOVE YOU.

A TEACHABLE HEART

"Be strong. Let us show ourselves to have strength of heart."
2 SAMUEL 10:12

Being brave means doing what God says. How do you know what God wants? Reading your Bible and praying will help you understand God's heart. Back in the garden of Eden, after Adam stepped out from his hiding place, God disciplined him. Remember that in Genesis 2 God told Adam not to eat from the tree of the knowledge of good and evil. Adam wasn't being brave when he just stood there while the devil was tempting Eve.

Obeying God and sticking up for what He wants is key to being brave. Another cool lesson is that a brave boy is one who has a teachable heart. Notice that Adam didn't argue with God. He knew he had messed up big-time. He listened as God told him how things were going to be.

Think about how you can make God the most important part of your life. Ask Him now to take over and direct all your steps.

I KNOW THAT THE ENEMY IS CONSTANTLY AT WORK TRYING TO CONVINCE ME THAT LAZINESS IS OKAY. HELP ME NOT TO BELIEVE HIM WHEN HE SAYS I AM WEAK. HIS GOAL IS TO DRAIN MY SPIRIT. HE WANTS HIS LIES TO FILL MY BEING SO THAT I WILL FEEL EMPTY. HELP ME TO REMEMBER WHO YOU SAY I AM, LORD.

WHAT'S BEST

"My ways are far beyond anything you could imagine."
ISAIAH 55:8 NLT

Sometimes you cannot get what you want. A brave young man will understand that God may have different plans for his life. Adam and Eve had it all, but because of their disobedience, God had to kick them out of the garden. This is the way life works, even today. Like Adam, you will have times when you find yourself making a bad choice. That's when you ask for forgiveness and ask God to help you be more like Jesus.

A brave person never forgets that God loves them. This truth helps them stay connected to God, no matter what the circumstances. Even in times when you don't feel like God is working in your life, let your faith keep your eyes open for His gentle leading.

Stay connected to God and let Him correct you. Stay humble and believe that He always wants what is best for you.

FATHER, I KNOW I HAVE AN ENEMY WHO WANTS ME TO BELIEVE THAT YOU ONLY ANSWER SOME OF MY PRAYERS SOME OF THE TIME. BUT I KNOW THAT YOU ARE HERE FOR ME ALL THE TIME. YOU DO SO MANY THINGS FOR ME THAT I CANNOT UNDERSTAND THEM ALL. THANK YOU FOR CALLING ME YOUR BELOVED CHILD.

STAY CLOSE

Come close to God and He will come close to you.
JAMES 4:8

A man named Enoch lived a very long time. The Bible says he walked faithfully with God. This is another way God defines bravery. You will find yourself tempted to do things that take up a lot of your time—hanging out with friends, playing video games, watching TV, texting. Not that those things are necessarily bad, but if they become super important, God will get pushed to the side.

Spending each day *with God* will help you do what's right. Make your quiet time with God the most important part of your day. Maybe you can ask your parents to wake you up a few minutes early each day so that you can read your Bible and talk to God. That would be a good way to go with God every day of your life.

Don't worry. Just stay close to the one who made you and follow Him.

ONE OF YOUR WONDERFUL NAMES IS YAHWEH. LORD. MASTER. ABSOLUTE RULER. THIS HELPS ME REMEMBER WHO I AM AS YOUR CHILD. YOU CREATED ME IN YOUR IMAGE. AS MY ALL-POWERFUL CREATOR, PLEASE REMIND ME THAT I AM ETERNALLY YOURS. HELP ME TO STICK UP FOR WHAT'S RIGHT. HELP ME TO BE BRAVE.

SPIRIT OF PRAISE

I will give them. . .a spirit of praise instead of a spirit of no hope.
ISAIAH 61:3

God wants you to live your life being brave. The Bible says that He gives you a spirit of praise. He wants you to look forward to all the exciting things He has for you each day. Having a spirit of praise means that you worship God by the choices you make and the example you set.

The world might leave you feeling like God isn't listening. It might make you feel hopeless some days. Becoming a brave leader means that your goal is to make God famous at school, at home, out on the playground—anywhere you go!

Do you pay attention to what God says is important? Reading your Bible every day will help you know what God feels about you and learn about all the ways He thinks you're special. Obeying Him will become your constant act of worship!

HELP ME SPEND MY TIME READING THE BIBLE AS MUCH AS I CAN SO I CAN KEEP MY HEART WRAPPED IN TRUTH. THE WORLD FINDS ITS POWER IN THE STRENGTH OF ITS ARMIES, BUT I PRAY THAT I WILL ALWAYS FIND MY STRENGTH IN THE POWER OF YOUR HOLY NAME, JESUS.

DO YOU BELIEVE?

Jesus said to them, "Do you have faith that I can do this?"
MATTHEW 9:28

A story in the Bible tells of two blind men who went to Jesus for healing. Jesus asked them a very important question: "Do you have faith that I can do this?" Without wasting a second, the men said, "Yes, Lord."

Being a brave young man means believing that Jesus is who He says He is and can do whatever He says He will do. You have to be like the blind men and seek Him out. Go to Jesus with a ton of faith and watch how God will start to use you in big ways.

What in your life is taking most of your time? Video games? Smartphone? Computer? TV? Friends? When spending time with Jesus is your number one answer, then you can feel confident that He will give you strength to stick up for what's right and be the leader you were made to be!

DON'T LET ME LOOK UP TO THE ONES WHO RELY ON THEMSELVES TO SOLVE THEIR PROBLEMS. HELP ME TO LET YOU BE IN CHARGE. I WANT TO FOLLOW YOUR WORDS, AND I KNOW THAT YOU WILL NEVER LET ME DOWN. BECAUSE YOU ARE MY MASTER, I WILL HAVE NO EXPECTATIONS OTHER THAN THE ONES ABOUT YOUR PERFECT PROMISES.

FIRST AND LAST

"He will not stop helping you."
1 CHRONICLES 28:20

Remember that Jesus was there for you yesterday, and He will be there for you today. When tomorrow comes, Jesus will be waiting for you. It's awesome that one of His names is *Alpha and Omega*, which means "the first and last." To become a brave boy, you have to decide to live your life for Jesus.

What does that look like? Picture a football field. The two parts of the field where touchdowns are scored are called end zones. If the player catches the ball outside of the end zone, the touchdown doesn't count. Making Jesus your Alpha and Omega means He goes before you and behind you. Like the end zones, He is at the beginning of your day and all the way at the other side at the end of your day.

Decide to stay in Jesus. When you do that, you can be confident that all your bravery will come from the one who loves you more than anything.

LORD JESUS, HELP ME TO TALK TO YOU WHEN I WAKE UP. PLEASE TEACH ME TO LISTEN TO YOU SO MY DAY WILL BE LIVED FOR YOU. GO BEFORE ME AND PROTECT ME. PLEASE HELP ME TO FINISH MY DAY BY PRAYING TO YOU. GIVE ME A THANKFUL HEART SO I CAN ALWAYS BE GRATEFUL FOR EVERYTHING YOU DO FOR ME!

LIKE THE KING

Everything you do should be done in love.
1 CORINTHIANS 16:14

Jesus is the King of kings! If you remember this and live each of your days praising Him, then bravery will become the trait that people know you by. One rule that Jesus followed all throughout His earthly ministry was that He did everything in love.

How do you treat your parents and teachers? How do you treat your friends? Doing everything you do in love means treating others with respect. It means not doing things out of selfishness. Acting in love looks like cleaning your room before your parents remind you to clean it. Acting in love looks like thinking of ways to help others.

Think about the times your mom and dad did something for you that filled your heart. It feels wonderful to be loved. The Bible says God is love and He made you in His image. Be a young man who wants to be like the King!

LORD, HELP ME TO REJECT EVERYTHING THAT GOES AGAINST YOUR LOVE FOR ME. NOTHING CAN TAKE YOU OFF YOUR THRONE OR AWAY FROM MY HEART. HELP ME TO THINK ABOUT OTHER PEOPLE. YOU ALONE ARE WORTHY. I PRAY THAT YOU WILL GO BEFORE ME TODAY AND SHOW ME HOW TO LOVE OTHERS LIKE YOU LOVE ME.

CHOICES

They knew they had been with Jesus.
ACTS 4:13

We make choices all day long. Asking Jesus how to behave is a great step in becoming a brave leader.

Being brave means doing the right thing even when no one is looking. It's also bravery to do the right thing, knowing that you're not going to get anything in return. Holding the door open for someone instead of having to be the first one in is a great way to show respect. If you're watching videos on YouTube and an inappropriate ad pops up, be brave and walk away.

Don't forget that God is always watching. He loves you and is cheering you on as you accomplish all the things He has set up for you to do. Whether you're at a friend's house or at home, make sure you choose to do what's right. You never know how your friends or family will grow closer to God because they saw you choose to act with integrity.

EL ELYON. GOD MOST HIGH. TODAY I WILL REMEMBER THAT I AM DEARLY LOVED AND FOREVER FORGIVEN. I HAVE BEEN SET FREE! THE CHAINS OF SIN HAVE BEEN DESTROYED, NOT BY THE HAMMER OF MAN, BUT BY JESUS. PLEASE HELP ME TO MAKE THE RIGHT CHOICES, EVEN WHEN IT'S REALLY HARD. THANK YOU, FATHER!

MY COMFORT

Your comfort brings joy to my soul.
PSALM 94:19

What makes you happy? Getting wrapped up in fun things like toys and games is easy, but take a minute and talk to God about His plan for your life. He wants you to have fun, but He also is training you up as a brave boy to one day become a brave man.

For now, as you ask God to lead you on the path of bravery, look for ways to be a light for Jesus. Don't forget that He is your comfort, which means He doesn't want you to feel stressed out. When things don't go your way, ask God to help. Jesus promises to give you rest.

Spend time today thinking about a way that God might be trying to use you to help His people. How can you put your talents to work to accomplish something life changing for His glory? You're on your way to a life that will lead people to Jesus!

GOD, HELP ME TO REMEMBER THAT I DON'T NEED TO TRY HARDER OR WORRY ABOUT GETTING APPROVAL FROM OTHER PEOPLE. I JUST NEED JESUS. THANK YOU FOR REMINDING ME THAT IN YOUR EYES I AM PRICELESS. PLEASE KEEP POURING YOUR GRACE OVER ME.

POWER AND LOVE

For God did not give us a spirit of fear. He gave us a
spirit of power and of love and of a good mind.
2 TIMOTHY 1:7

Because there are so many scary things in the world, worrying can become a habit. But being a brave boy means that you believe God every time He says don't worry. The Bible is clear on how God wants you to be confident and brave.

One thing that God has given you is a spirit of power. If you've seen any superhero movies or read comic books, you know what make-believe power looks like. The Hulk is a massive force to be reckoned with. But God gives you spiritual power to be brave and strong for real. Another gift God gives is a spirit of love. Like Jesus, being brave is sharing His love with others.

Finally, God has given you a spirit of a good mind. He has gifted you with the ability to think about things from His perspective. After you spend time in His Word, you can begin to think about plans to be a brave blessing to others.

FATHER, A LOT OF PEOPLE IN MY LIFE DO NOT HAVE A RELATIONSHIP WITH JESUS. I PRAY FOR THEM. PLEASE SHOW THEM HOW GRACIOUS YOU ARE. SEND ME TO THE HEARTS OF MANY WHO ARE HURTING AND WEAK. GUIDE ME TO THEM AND HELP ME TO TELL THEM ABOUT THEIR COMING KING, JESUS THE MESSIAH.

THAT'S A PROMISE

We can trust God that He will do what He promised.
HEBREWS 10:23

God is a promise keeper. Let's take a look at a few people who trusted that God would keep His word and make them brave.

Moses was brave. God called him to lead the Israelites out of Egypt. That was a ton of people, and at first Moses didn't think he could do it. He even asked God to choose his brother to do the job. But Moses finally believed that God was big enough and became a brave leader of many people.

Or how about Joseph? Joseph was sold by his brothers into slavery. For years he went through bad situations (even found himself in prison) before God brought him up to a very high position. God used the hard times to help Joseph become brave.

We can't forget Jesus! You know all the horrible things that happened to Him. He paid the ultimate price by giving up His life on the cross. So remember, keep trusting God and ask Him to make you braver each day.

DEAR JESUS, I KNOW THAT YOU ARE MY SOURCE OF STRENGTH. BY YOUR POWER YOU WILL BREAK THE ENEMY'S LIES HE SPEAKS TO ME. JESUS, YOU ARE LIKE A ROD OF STRONGEST IRON THAT YOU WILL USE TO DASH THE DEVIL'S SCHEMES TO PIECES AS IF THEY WERE FORMED OF BRITTLE CLAY. I TRUST YOU TODAY!

FOR REAL

For by His loving-favor you have been saved from the punishment of sin through faith. It is not by anything you have done. It is a gift of God.
EPHESIANS 2:8

Birthdays are special. Isn't it fun to have all of your friends and family make a big deal about you? Isn't it a great feeling to know that people care about you and want to celebrate the day you were born? God loves you every day like it's your birthday because He is the one who created you!

There is only one *you*! As you read your Bible and study all the ways God used normal people to be brave and do great things, pray about how you can use the gifts He has given you. There will never be another *you*, so be encouraged to know that you are very, very special.

The best gift of all is the gift Jesus gave you when you asked for Him to become Lord over your life. That's called salvation, and it was free! Isn't God great? Brave people praise God as they go and tell others about this awesome gift!

LORD, I KNOW THAT YOU GAVE ME LIFE AND OPENED THE EYES OF MY HEART TO BE ABLE TO SEE JESUS FOR WHO HE REALLY IS. GIVE ME A CHANCE TO TELL OTHERS HOW THEY CAN HAVE THE SAME GIFT OF REAL LIFE THROUGH JESUS. LET MY WORDS AND ACTIONS SHOW PEOPLE HOW WONDERFUL YOU ARE!

GIFT OF LIFE

"But He knows the way that I take.
When He has tried me, I will come out as gold."
JOB 23:10

Today is a gift. It's easy to get stuck in a routine and forget your purpose. The enemy wants God's children to forget how important they are and get stuck complaining about all the things that are not right. Jesus knew that things weren't always going to be easy, and He was brave. He found ways to love people and let them know they mattered.

Today is a gift. What talents has God given you? What are you really good at? Think about using those skills to be brave. If you have sports practice, give it everything you have and be respectful to your coaches. If you are working on a project for school, give it all you have and do your best.

Today is a gift from the one who thinks you're really special. Enjoy it. Become even braver and do your best job ever telling your friends who Jesus is. You won't regret it!

GOD, HELP ME TO LIVE EACH MOMENT OF THIS NEW DAY YOU'VE GIVEN ME WITH A SERVANT HEART. BE MY EXAMPLE. I KNOW THAT YOU CAREFULLY AND LOVINGLY MADE ME. I DON'T WANT TO TAKE MY LIFE FOR GRANTED. HELP ME TO SHOW COMPASSION TO SOMEONE WHO NEEDS TO KNOW YOUR LOVE.

GRACE

"I am with you always, even to the end of the world."
MATTHEW 28:20

Being brave means understanding God's grace. He loves you so much that He sent Jesus to save you. And not only did He save you, but Jesus promises to be right there with you forever. That's pretty awesome. Whether your day is filled with sunshine or rain, it's really great to know that you are not alone.

Whatever today brings, you can be confident that God is taking care of you. He sees what you're going through, and He will make a way to guide your steps. Being brave means trusting that God will always be on your side.

How can you practice bravery? Decide right now that God is with you and that sticking up for what's right is your goal. Be the example that people around you look up to. Be the young man who spends his life making God known. Tell others that God loves them and that His grace changes lives.

FATHER, THANK YOU FOR BEING RIGHT BY MY SIDE. YOU WON'T LET ME FACE TODAY ALONE. YOU GO BEFORE ME AND STAND BEHIND ME. THE PROBLEMS IN LIFE ARE TEMPORARY, AND THEY CERTAINLY AREN'T MY PURPOSE. THEY WILL PASS, AND WHEN THEY DO, I'LL KNOW WITHOUT A DOUBT THAT YOU WERE THE ONE WHO SOLVED THEM.

SERVE

The Holy Spirit helps us where we are weak.
ROMANS 8:26

Having the right attitude about things will help you on your journey to becoming a brave boy. You know there are days when your mom or dad asks you to do something and you have that *not now* feeling. You'd rather keep playing or hanging out with your friend than help set the table for dinner. You'd rather watch funny videos on YouTube than clean your room.

Being brave means living for God. It sounds simple, but you know how easy it is for life to get in the way. Some days it might feel like a million distractions fill your mind. This makes it hard to concentrate on the things God has for you.

Decide now that you are ready to be a brave young man who wants to serve God. Capture that *Yes, now!* attitude and watch how much God uses you!

KEEP MY HEART ROOTED IN YOU, LORD. YOU ARE WORTHY OF EVERY OUNCE OF MY LIFE. HELP ME TO SERVE YOU TODAY. THANK YOU FOR WANTING WHAT IS BEST FOR ME. PLEASE OPEN MY EYES TO NEW WAYS I CAN MAKE A DIFFERENCE IN THE WORLD TODAY. HELP ME TO PUT A SMILE ON A FRIEND'S FACE. ALL FOR YOUR GLORY!

SACRIFICE

"Be strong and have strength of heart! Do not be afraid or lose faith. For the Lord your God is with you anywhere you go."
JOSHUA 1:9

If you want to be brave, you need to think about Jesus. He did so many brave things, but the biggest thing was going to the cross. Jesus became a sacrifice for us so that our sins could be forgiven. More than time, money, and possessions, Jesus gave up His life for us.

Can you think of something you'd be willing to give up to make God famous? Jesus actually calls us to give up our lives to live for Him. That might sound confusing, but it is a very simple command. Becoming a brave boy means reading your Bible and obeying what God says.

Decide that today is the day you will become more like Jesus and live your life for Him! Read His Word and ask Him to show you ways that you can change. Then your light will shine even brighter, and when people ask you about your bravery, you can tell them all about Jesus!

I WANT TO REMEMBER THAT YOU ARE HERE WITH ME AND THAT YOU ARE FOR ME. YOU ALONE ARE MY DELIVERER. THERE ARE DAYS WHEN I DOUBT THIS. FORGIVE ME. I KNOW THAT YOU DON'T LOVE ME ANY LESS. HELP ME TO THINK ABOUT JESUS AND THE SACRIFICE HE MADE FOR ME!

BE STILL

"The Lord will fight for you. All you have to do is keep still."
EXODUS 14:14

Moses was a great example of a brave person. God called him to lead the Israelites out of Egypt. They were being mistreated by the pharaoh and held as slaves. Moses was nervous to have to talk to the pharaoh, but he did it knowing that God had given him this special and important job.

In the Bible story, the Israelites had been set free. But the Egyptian army pursued them, and they found themselves hemmed in by the Red Sea. They couldn't turn around, but how were they going to cross the sea? With the angry Egyptian soldiers bearing down on them, things looked hopeless.

Moses had to remind them that God was in charge. That's what brave people do. They trust that God is big enough to do what He says. That's "God fighting for you." Brave people use that trust to obey Him. That's the "being still" part. In the story, God parted the waters so His people could cross to safety. God will do the same for you!

GOD, PLEASE LEAD ME TODAY. SOME DAYS IT'S HARD TO KNOW THAT YOU ARE HERE WITH ME. THANK YOU FOR THE STORY OF MOSES. YOU TAUGHT HIM HOW TO BE BRAVE, AND HE DID BIG THINGS. I WANT THAT FOR MY LIFE TOO. HOLD ME CLOSE. SHOW ME HOW TO BE STILL LONG ENOUGH TO HEAR YOU SPEAK. I LOVE YOU!

FOLLOW ME

*Jesus called out to them, "Come, follow me,
and I will show you how to fish for people!"*
MATTHEW 4:19 NLT

Brave people know who their leader is. Believers know that Jesus is their leader because of His promise to be with them always. As you continue in your training to become a young man with integrity, follow Jesus by doing what He says is important to Him.

One big job Jesus has for you is to become fishers of people. That might sound strange, but what Jesus means is that His children will go out and tell others about what He has done. Maybe you've heard people talk about sharing the gospel. This means telling people how Jesus died for them and that He loves them.

Being brave isn't always easy, but it's always right. A lot of people in your life need to know Jesus. God is proud of you. Keep being the best brave leader you can be, and never stop following Jesus.

LET YOUR WORDS MAKE ME BRAVE. LET THEM CARRY MY HEART THROUGH EVERY SITUATION I ENCOUNTER. LET YOUR TRUTH BE THE STRONG HANDS THAT LIFT ME OUT OF CONFUSION AND SET ME DOWN ON THE ROCK OF JESUS CHRIST. KEEP ME ON THE PATH YOU'VE CHOSEN SPECIFICALLY FOR ME. YOU ARE THE LORD, AND I PRAISE YOU.

NOTHING!

Nothing can keep us from the love of God.
ROMANS 8:38

Brave people who love Jesus live each day knowing that nothing happens that will cause God to leave them alone. They understand that even though they may make mistakes, asking forgiveness and continuing to worship God is the way to move forward.

If you get sick, God is still with you. If you have to move to a new house, God still loves you. If you get a bad grade on your report card, God is still proud of you. Knowing that nothing can change the way God feels about you should give you confidence.

God used a man in the Bible named Paul to tell a lot of people about God's love. Paul wasn't perfect, but he was very brave. He let the confidence that God gave him motivate him not to worry about what people thought. Paul kept telling people about Jesus. You can do the same. God thinks you're something special.

GOD, PLEASE WALK THROUGH TODAY WITH ME. HELP ME TO STAY RIGHT WHERE YOU NEED ME. KEEP ME SAFE. PLEASE KEEP SHOWING ME GRACE. THANK YOU FOR FORGIVING ME. KEEP BEING MY SHIELD, AND KEEP LIFTING MY HEAD HIGH. EVERY TIME I CALL TO YOU, I KNOW THAT YOU WILL ANSWER. HELP ME TO FOLLOW YOUR WILL FOR MY LIFE.

GO!

*Those who are right with God have as
much strength of heart as a lion.*
PROVERBS 28:1

Your strength doesn't come from trying harder. Your strength comes from praying harder. Your worth doesn't come from doing more work. Your worth comes from God. If you want to become brave, start by believing God and what He says about you. That's what builds confidence. Confidence builds character, and that's what all the brave people in the Bible had.

The Bible tells of a brave boy named David who helped his father tend the family's sheep. That doesn't seem like too exciting of a job, but David did his best and obeyed. The Bible says that David was strong and even killed a lion and a bear that tried to get his sheep! Those skills came in handy later on when he faced the Philistine giant Goliath and killed him with just a single stone.

God eventually made David king. It doesn't matter where you live, God will make you brave and give you good things to do. Let your strength come from Him. Go and be amazed at what you will be able to do for His glory.

GOD, I KNOW THAT YOU ARE THE ONE WHO MAKES ME BRAVE. HELP ME TO BE A BRAVER BOY TODAY THAN I WAS YESTERDAY. NO MATTER WHAT I'M DOING, PLEASE TEACH ME.

BE A LIGHT

Live and work without pride.
EPHESIANS 4:2

Jesus is calling you to be a light. This means that your life can be used to lead people to Him. This happens when you make good choices and work hard. When you have integrity—doing the right thing even when no one is looking—people start to notice you. They begin to see that there's something different about you.

Being a light for Jesus means not being prideful. Pride is when people give themselves, instead of God, all the credit. Brave boys give God all the credit. Ask Him to show you areas in your life where you might be prideful. Then, with His help, you can work hard at changing those behaviors, and your light will shine brighter.

The best part of shining bright in a world that likes to be selfish is that you get to talk to people about important things. Be brave and show people how awesome Jesus is.

LORD, YOU ARE MY HOLY FATHER. HELP ME NOT TO BE PRIDEFUL SO I CAN HELP GIVE YOU THE GLORY. I KNOW THAT THERE IS NOTHING MY HEART SHOULD EVER FEAR. EVEN THOUGH I CAN'T SEE YOU, PLEASE STAND GUARD OVER MY LIFE. PLEASE KEEP HELPING ME CHANGE MY SELFISH WAYS. I LOVE YOU.

ASK

God is faithful.
1 CORINTHIANS 10:13

Don't be shy. Tell God what is on your heart. He loves to hear your voice. Even though He knows what you need, the Bible says ask anyway. The Creator of everything is there to take care of you. He wants to make sure that you have everything you need. That's why He sent Jesus to you.

Sometimes God may not give you what you ask for. That doesn't mean He doesn't care. It means He has something better for you.

Jesus is your life. Make choices like He did. That's the key to brave living. His whole life was built on sacrifice. Give away your time. Maybe that means listening to a friend who needs help. Jesus made sure He always prayed and did His Father's will. He put others first all the time. Jesus even gave up His life so that others could be saved. God is on your side!

GOD, PLEASE WATCH OVER ME. I'M ASKING YOU TO PLEASE HELP ME TO BE MORE LIKE JESUS. HELP ME TO BE BRAVE AND TO SAY NO TO BAD CHOICES. ALWAYS SURROUND ME WITH YOUR LOVE, FORGIVENESS, AND HOPE. HELP ME ALWAYS TO LISTEN TO YOUR VOICE AND OBEY WHAT YOU SAY. TEACH ME WHAT TO ASK FOR.

TRUE

Jesus spoke to them and said,
"Take hope. It is I. Do not be afraid!"
MATTHEW 14:27

Brave people love Jesus, and they know that what He says is true. Thinking about all the lessons He taught will help you rise above all the distractions in life.

Jesus was with His friends when a great crowd arrived. The people were hungry. The friends tried to send them away so they could find food. They only had two fish and five loaves of bread.

Be brave and try to do the best in everything you do. Jesus is there with you. He told His friends to bring Him the little food they had. Jesus had the crowd sit. There's a good reminder there. Take some of your quiet time to rest with Jesus. That's when Jesus did a miracle and made so much food out of so little. That's what He will do with your confidence. He will turn you into a superbrave young man as you spend more and more time with Him.

AS I HEAD OUT INTO THIS NEW DAY, HELP ME TO REMEMBER THAT ALL OF YOUR WORDS ARE TRUE. GIVE ME COURAGEOUS FAITH. DELIVER ME FROM MY SELFISHNESS. STRIKE DOWN MY FEARS. THANK YOU FOR BLESSING ME. I WILL BE BRAVE BECAUSE YOU ARE MY RIGHTEOUS GOD AND I LOVE YOU.

STAND UP

"Do not be afraid, just believe."
MARK 5:36

God is growing you into a very brave boy. He knows how wonderful you are, and He also sees where you're going. He is constantly giving you the tools to become a strong leader. You might not think that someone your age could lead, but that's not true.

In your classroom, you are leader every time you follow your teacher's directions. The other kids in your class will notice. Sometimes it's hard to do the right thing. Do it anyway. At home let your bravery show in the way you help around the house without being asked. Don't let laziness keep you from greatness.

Don't be afraid to be the only one who sticks up for what is right. Don't be afraid to help the person no one else wants to help. Don't be afraid to let someone else go first. You are important to Jesus, and He is the one who is making you brave.

GOD, SHOW ME WAYS I CAN PRACTICE BEING BRAVE. LET ME BE THE ONE WHO STANDS UP FOR WHAT IS RIGHT. HELP ME TO BE AN EXAMPLE TO MY FRIENDS OF WHAT A JESUS FOLLOWER LOOKS LIKE. TAKE MY DAYS AND SHOW ME HOW TO STAND STRONG IN THE FACE OF CHANGE. THANK YOU FOR LOVING ME.

DOORS

May the Lord Jesus Christ be with your spirit.
May you have God's loving-favor.
2 TIMOTHY 4:22

Some days it's hard not to feel tired. You'd rather stay in bed when your parents say it's time to get up. You'd rather watch TV than do your chores. When you find yourself in such a situation, remember that God is training you up to be a brave boy.

Ask Jesus to motivate you to shine. Ask Him to open doors of opportunity so that you will have many chances to practice doing the right thing. Don't forget that Jesus is with you. God loves you very much, and He helps you all the time.

Take every chance to lead. Look around for people who need a word of encouragement, and say something nice to them. Look for someone to help, and let them know that Jesus loves them. These are just a few ways to practice being brave. God has great plans for your life!

LORD, I WANT TO DO YOUR WILL. SHOW ME HOW I CAN BE MORE LIKE YOU. I WANT TO BE BRAVE. I ALWAYS WANT TO TRY MY BEST TO HELP PEOPLE AND BE A GOOD FRIEND. THANK YOU FOR LOVING ME. KEEP ME SAFE AND HELP ME TO WANT WHAT YOU WANT.

POWERFUL

*"Do not be afraid of them. Remember the Lord
Who is great and honored with fear."*
NEHEMIAH 4:14

Your life is special because you are a child of God. He will take care of you and make sure all your needs are met. He is your heavenly Father who has great things in store for your life. Follow His commands. That will keep you on the right path.

The most important first step you can take today is to decide to put God first. That's what brave people do. No matter what happens, let your entire day honor God. That's the way you will replace selfishness with praise. That's the way you will worship God.

Keep reading your Bible. Remember that it says the Word of God is sharper than a double-edged sword. A sword is a very powerful weapon. Bible study will help you arm yourself with truth and will also help keep you connected to Jesus. Let Him teach you about bravery. What an exciting time it is to be loved by Jesus!

LORD, I THINK ABOUT HOW IT'S HARD SOMETIMES TO DO THE RIGHT THING. I PRAY THAT YOU'LL HELP ME TO BE MORE UNSELFISH AND HELP ME TO FIND WAYS TO SERVE MY FAMILY. I REALLY WANT TO BE MORE OF A GIVER. SHOW ME HOW TO BE MORE LIKE JESUS AND USE MY TIME TO BE A BLESSING TO OTHERS.

RIGHT ON TIME

Now the God Who helps you not to give up and gives you strength will help you think so you can please each other as Christ Jesus did.
ROMANS 15:5

Some days you will feel like you're all alone. Remember that you're not. Being brave means having the faith to know that God doesn't go back on His promises. He tells us that He will never leave us. He also says that nothing can pull us away from Jesus.

The enemy doesn't want you to become brave. He wants you to feel lonely and afraid. Jesus had a friend named Lazarus. Lazarus became ill and passed away, and his sisters sent for Jesus to help. Jesus took His time getting to the town where His friend was buried. Our God is love, and Jesus knew that He would help His friends.

When Jesus arrived in the town of Bethany, the sisters chastised Jesus, saying that their brother wouldn't have died if Jesus had gotten there sooner. Deeply moved in spirit, Jesus cried, but then He performed a miracle, raising Lazarus from the dead!

LORD, HELP ME TO BE OKAY WITH YOUR PLANS FOR MY LIFE. I KNOW THEY ARE SO MUCH BETTER THAN ANYTHING I COULD WISH FOR. SOMETIMES I FEEL SAD BECAUSE I'VE PRAYED FOR THINGS THAT I NEVER GET. FORGIVE ME FOR BEING SELFISH. HELP ME TO GAIN CONFIDENCE TO KNOW THAT YOU ARE ALWAYS RIGHT ON TIME!

HANG IN THERE

I will be glad and rejoice in your unfailing love, for you have seen my troubles, and you care about the anguish of my soul.
PSALM 31:7 NLT

You're important to God. He loves you so much. If you ever feel like you can't possibly become a brave boy, hang in there, and look a little more closely at the story of Joseph.

Joseph had some brothers who didn't like him too much. When he was young, Joseph received a beautiful coat from his father. This made his brothers jealous. Then Joseph had a dream and told his family that one day they would bow down to him. This made them mad, so they sold him to slave traders.

Joseph was taken to Egypt where he was sold to the pharaoh. Then more bad stuff happened to Joseph, and he was put in prison for a crime he didn't commit! Can you imagine? But God knows what He's doing. Joseph stayed brave, and eventually the pharaoh put him in charge of Egypt! That's what God is doing in your life. He's taking the normal, everyday routines and turning them into something spectacular.

LORD, I REALLY NEED HELP WAITING. I REALLY NEED HELP HAVING A STRONG FAITH. I WANT TO BE BRAVE, BUT SOMETIMES IT'S HARD NOT TO BE DISAPPOINTED. KEEP MY EYES ON YOU. KEEP MY MIND ON YOUR WORD. HELP ME TO WORSHIP YOU INSTEAD OF WORRYING ABOUT THE THINGS I CAN'T CHANGE!

STARTING LINE

Let us keep running in the race that God has planned for us.
HEBREWS 12:1

God is training you up in the way of bravery and integrity. He is proud of how far you have come in your walk with Him. Keep taking your Bible study seriously. Keep praying. Don't stop trusting God. Don't let the enemy tell you that unanswered prayers mean that God doesn't care.

Picture yourself at the starting line of a long-distance race. The competitors are bouncing up and down with nervous energy waiting for the sign to start running. Then it's time to take off, and everyone starts moving in the same direction. After a while, the crowd thins, and the faster people go to the front, while the slower ones drift toward the back.

The smart runners pace themselves. Your spiritual walk is the same way. Pacing yourself looks like trusting God no matter what. Don't stop being brave just because you feel tired. Don't drift away just because your prayer hasn't been answered. Keep going. God is right there with you!

LORD, I FEEL LIKE IT'S EASY TO LOSE TRACK OF WHERE I'M SUPPOSED TO GO. I'M READING MY BIBLE AND HAVING MY QUIET TIME WITH YOU, BUT I STILL SEEM TO BELIEVE THAT I HAVEN'T DONE THE RIGHT THINGS TO KEEP ME RUNNING AFTER YOU. HELP ME TO LISTEN MORE. LEAD ME, AND KEEP SHOWING ME THE WAY.

LISTEN

*"I called out to the Lord because of my
trouble, and He answered me."*
JONAH 2:2

Being brave when everyone around you isn't might feel weird, but don't worry. God is with you, so you can't mess anything up. Be strong. Do your best to pray for God's help, and then listen for His direction. There will be times when you might be the only one doing the right thing. That's okay.

God made a man named Jonah in the Bible brave. Jonah went to a big, scary place where he didn't want to go to. He went there to tell the people about God and how their lives could be so much better if they asked God to take over. Jonah was the only one who stood up for God, and many people listened to what he had to say.

But it wasn't easy. At first Jonah tried running away from God. He didn't want to be brave. He thought avoiding the hard things in life was the answer. Eventually Jonah obeyed, and an entire city was saved.

LORD, I WANT TO BE A BETTER LISTENER. I TALK ALL DAY LONG. WHEN I'M WITH YOU, HELP ME TO HEAR WHAT YOU HAVE TO SAY TO ME. I HAVE SO MANY DISTRACTIONS IN LIFE, AND SOMETIMES I FEEL LIKE YOU'RE FAR AWAY OR YOU DON'T UNDERSTAND WHAT I'M GOING THROUGH. FORGIVE ME, AND TELL ME WHAT IS ON YOUR HEART.

GOD IS ENOUGH

Be strong with the Lord's strength.
EPHESIANS 6:10

Abraham was very brave. God used him to be a blessing for many people. One thing that made Abraham brave was that he was obedient. God called Abraham to leave his family and move to a faraway land. Abraham was seventy-five years old when he left!

Being brave means trusting that God is with you and wants the best for you. Even if you don't have all the answers, living each day knowing that God is enough is all you need to be a brave young boy. What is God calling you to do that seems a little scary? Don't forget that He will go with you every step of the way.

God loves you. He thinks you are something special. You are His, and nothing will change that truth. Go to the people and places to which God is calling you, and be thankful that He is making you braver each day.

LORD, HELP ME TO OBEY YOU THE FIRST TIME, JUST LIKE ABRAHAM DID. EVEN IF I DON'T FEEL LIKE IT, PLEASE HELP ME TO REMEMBER HOW MUCH I MEAN TO YOU. I WANT MY OBEDIENCE TO YOU TO BE A FORM OF WORSHIP. THANK YOU FOR LOVING ME. THANK YOU FOR CARING ABOUT ME. I'M READY TO FOLLOW YOU WHEREVER YOU LEAD.

FEELING BLUE

"I know that You can do all things.
Nothing can put a stop to Your plans."
JOB 42:2

If you ever feel sad, that's okay. Feeling blue doesn't mean you're not brave. Many brave people in the Bible went through tough times. Job was a man who knew hard times. The devil tried to make his life miserable and even told God that he thought Job would stop trusting God.

Job lost everything. He was sad. Depressed. Tired. Angry. You name it, Job felt it. To make things worse, Job had some friends who accused him of sinning and told him that he got what he deserved. They even told him to give up and forget God. That was the last thing Job needed to do, because God was all he had.

Fast-forward to the end of the book of Job, and you'll see that Job never stopped trusting God. No matter how bad things got, Job kept holding on to God. He realized that God could do anything, and nothing could stop Him. And finally, the Bible says that God gave Job twice as much as he had lost!

GOD, PLEASE FILL MY HEART. I FEEL DOWN SOMETIMES, AND I DON'T LIKE IT. THANK YOU FOR THE STORY OF JOB. IT HELPS ME KNOW THAT YOU WILL NEVER LEAVE ME. IT HELPS ME REMEMBER THAT YOU HAVE MADE ME BRAVE AND STRONG. YOU HAVE ALSO MADE ME PATIENT. THANK YOU FOR THIS NEW DAY!

GOLDEN RULE

"Do to others as you would like them to do to you."
LUKE 6:31 NLT

Brave people treat others the way they want to be treated. Maybe you've heard of the Golden Rule. Jesus explained what that meant to His close friends, the disciples.

Jesus knew His disciples had to be brave, so He taught them important lessons that would help them stay strong. First, Jesus told them to do good to people who didn't like them. He said to pray for those who hurt them. He also told them to give without expecting anything in return.

Jesus went on to say that there's a reward for those who act like God's children by loving those who are against them. He said to be compassionate or to care about others like God does. But how can you do all of those things? Only with the help of Jesus. He doesn't love you less if you forget to obey His directions. He knows that with Him on your side, you will be able to do more than you know!

LORD, IT DOESN'T FEEL GOOD WHEN PEOPLE SAY HURTFUL THINGS. I'M ASKING THAT YOU WOULD HELP ME TO BE BRAVE AND REMIND ME TO PRAY FOR THEM. SHOW ME HOW TO LOVE THEM LIKE YOU DO. THANK YOU FOR FORGIVING ME WHEN I MESS UP. HELP ME TO CARE MORE ABOUT OTHERS.

WHERE ARE YOU?

Then the LORD God called to the man, "Where are you?"
GENESIS 3:9 NLT

At times you may feel like nothing goes your way. Don't worry. Things will change. God will always help you. Always. He is a promise keeper. Even from the very beginning of the Bible, you can see this trait at work. God rescues His children from those moments when things seem out of control.

Adam and Eve were the first people God created. He made the beautiful garden of Eden for their home. God let Adam name the animals, and all creatures lived without fear. Adam and Eve loved God. Remember, they only had that one rule: they were not to eat of the tree of the knowledge of good and evil.

But they were tempted by the devil to do the wrong thing. We have already mentioned that they did what they were told not to do. They disobeyed God and were sad. They tried hiding from God, but He pursued them and helped them. God does the same for you.

I FEEL LIKE HIDING SOMETIMES. I FEEL LIKE I'VE LET YOU DOWN, GOD. I CERTAINLY DON'T FEEL BRAVE WHEN THIS HAPPENS. HELP ME TO REMEMBER THE STORY OF ADAM AND EVE. YOU DIDN'T LET THEM GO. YOU WENT AND FOUND THEM AND SAVED THEM FROM THEIR SIN. THANK YOU, JESUS, FOR DOING THE SAME FOR ME!

EVERY WORD

*"People do not live by bread alone, but by
every word that comes from the mouth of God."*
MATTHEW 4:4 NLT

Do you know someone who loves to read? Maybe that's you! In any case, being brave requires you to be a reader of God's Word. Jesus even reminds us of that in the Bible. You might be familiar with the story, but it's important to reread it every now and then.

Jesus was about to begin His earthly ministry. He had been baptized and went out into the desert for forty days and nights. He fasted during this time and was very hungry. That's when the devil showed up to tempt Jesus to do the wrong thing. He told Jesus to turn some stones into loaves of bread so He could satisfy His hunger. Jesus refused.

He said that people don't just live on bread, but they need to live on every word of God. The Bible is a source of spiritual nutrition for everyone like you who is trying to become brave. Read it and live a brave life.

LORD, HELP ME TO READ MY BIBLE AND HELP ME TO APPLY WHAT I LEARN.
SHOW ME HOW TO BECOME BRAVER EACH DAY BY FOLLOWING YOUR RULES
FOR MY LIFE. I FEEL BETTER KNOWING THAT YOU ARE THE ONE IN CHARGE.
OPEN MY EYES TO SEE PEOPLE THE WAY YOU SEE THEM. THANK YOU!

BIG GOD

"So are My ways higher than your ways."
ISAIAH 55:9

We serve a very big God. His creation is mind blowing. From all the different kinds of animals to all the magnificent things in nature, it's clear to see that God is awesome. But out of all the amazing parts of creation, He made people in His image. That is something hard to imagine.

You are special. There aren't enough pages to fill a book that could hold all the ways to describe how much God loves you. From all the stars and galaxies, to all the people on earth, God made you unique. You are the only you. He gave you a special skill to use to bless others. Being brave means using that skill and changing the world for God's glory.

Take some time and write down all the ways God has blessed you. Is there a way you can begin to use any of them to make Him famous?

GOD, SOME DAYS I FEEL TINY, SMALL AND OUT OF SIGHT. I FEEL LIKE YOU'RE WAY OUT THERE IN THE BIG AND DARK UNIVERSE, TOO FAR AWAY TO SEE ME AND WHAT I'M GOING THROUGH. REMIND ME THAT YOU NEVER LEAVE ME AND THAT I MATTER. SHOW ME HOW I CAN USE THE GIFTS YOU'VE GIVEN ME TO BE A BLESSING TO OTHERS.

SAVED

Since God is for us, who can be against us?
ROMANS 8:31

The God of everything is on your side! That is all the encouragement you need to keep on being brave. Picture Him cheering you on in everything. Don't forget, He made you. He knows every part of you. God doesn't make mistakes. Don't let your mistakes define you.

A great Bible story tells about a woman who people made fun of because she made bad choices. It was so bad, she had to get water from the well in the heat of day to avoid the other women who would call her names. That's when Jesus found her. He comforted her and told her that He was the answer to all her problems.

After she met Jesus, she wound up telling her friends about Him, and many believed. The people begged Jesus to stay with them. So for two days he stayed and talked to them. That's when they knew that He was the Savior of the world. The woman knew Jesus was on her side, and she bravely shared His name!

I FEEL LIKE I DON'T FIT IN SOMETIMES. JESUS, I PRAY THAT YOU WOULD HELP ME TO FOCUS ON YOU. HELP ME NOT TO LET MY MISTAKES DEFINE ME. REMIND ME THAT YOU ARE HERE TO ENCOURAGE ME.

YES!

"Have strength of heart and do it."
EZRA 10:4

You will learn about many people who are brave. Some, like David and Joseph, fill a lot of pages of your Bible; others, like Esther and Rahab, not so many. Either way, when it comes to being strong and sticking up for God, the only thing that matters is that you try.

One attack on your hard work of being brave is the enemy's lies. Just as he lied to Adam and Eve in the Garden of Eden, he lies to you about your worth. Just as he lied to Jesus in the desert, the enemy lies to you about your strength.

Don't worry about what you don't have. The enemy knows all the amazing things you can do for God's glory. Don't let his lies keep you from being brave and accomplishing what God made you to do. Don't worry. Just say yes!

LORD, I LOOK AROUND AND SEE HOW SOME OF MY FRIENDS HAVE A LOT MORE THAN I DO. HELP ME NOT TO COMPARE MYSELF TO OTHERS. PLEASE KEEP ME ON THE STRAIGHT PATH. KEEP MY EYES ON YOU. SHOW ME HOW TO BE BRAVE NO MATTER WHAT SITUATION I'M IN. HELP ME TO SAY YES TO ALL YOUR COMMANDS.

CHANGED

We have God's power.
2 CORINTHIANS 6:7

Thinking of others is a great way to be brave. Maybe you've had a teacher in school who had the students say something kind about someone else. Maybe your parents have had you make a birthday card for a brother or sister, grandparent, or aunt or uncle. Lifting other people up is a powerful tool in living like Jesus.

A wonderful story in the Bible tells of Jesus meeting a man who was very sick. He couldn't walk. In fact, the Bible says he had been ill for thirty-eight years. Jesus saw the man and approached him. He wanted to make the man better.

After Jesus asked if he wanted to be healed, the man said he couldn't get into a nearby pool people were entering to be cured. Jesus told the man to get up, and the man did! Jesus gave the man a miracle, and his life was forever changed. Who can you give a kind word to today?

JESUS, I HOPE THAT I CAN KEEP PRACTICING BRAVERY BY SPEAKING KIND WORDS TO PEOPLE. GIVE ME CHANCES TO SAY THINGS THAT WILL UPLIFT OTHERS. IT'S HARD TO KNOW WHAT TO SAY WHEN A FRIEND IS SAD, BUT I PRAY THAT YOU WILL SHOW ME HOW TO SPEAK TRUTH. USE ME TO REMIND PEOPLE THAT YOU ARE THERE FOR THEM.

FURTHER

*"The Lord has sent me so you might be able to
see again and be filled with the Holy Spirit."*
ACTS 9:17

The best part of being brave is that your confidence takes you further than you ever thought you could go. That's what happened to a man named Saul. God took his old life and turned it into something amazing. Saul went from a small town called Tarsus to the ends of the Roman Empire because he was being brave for God.

Saul was a very smart man who in the beginning didn't like people who loved Jesus. He was against them. He didn't believe in Jesus. But God believed that He could use someone like Saul to change the world.

One day Saul was journeying to Damascus to arrest God's people and take them to prison, when suddenly a light from heaven flashed around him and he fell to the ground and heard Jesus calling his name! After this happened, Saul's life changed. People even began calling him by a new name—Paul. He began loving Jesus more than anything, and he made four long journeys to share the message of God's love with untold numbers of people.

LORD, I PRAY THAT YOU WOULD OPEN MY EYES IN A WAY THAT WOULD
HELP ME TO SEE PEOPLE AS YOU DO. I WANT TO GROW AND BE BRAVE
LIKE PAUL, TELLING AS MANY PEOPLE ABOUT YOU AS I CAN.

MY HELPER

My help comes from the Lord, Who made heaven and earth.
PSALM 121:2

What a relief to know that God watches over you. There's nowhere you can go where God can't see you. Besides, He thinks the world of you. He is always guarding your life. He is always with you. God made all the stars in the sky, and He made the oceans. He made the mountains, and He made you. That's pretty amazing.

If God made everything, He can surely help you on your journey to becoming a brave young man. Keep praying and making time to listen. Trust that God is always with you. Don't stop to second-guess God. Don't waste time thinking that God has left you alone to go help someone else. He promises not to let you stumble.

The hard times won't last, but God's love for you goes on forever. Rest in the goodness of His will. Keep walking with Him, and practice being brave. Follow Him and be blessed.

I NEED HELP, JESUS. I THINK I'M DOING THE RIGHT THING, BUT THEN I MESS UP AND FEEL BAD. I DON'T WANT YOU TO BE UPSET WITH ME. I KNOW THAT YOU ARE A GOD OF GRACE AND THERE'S NOTHING I COULD DO THAT WOULD MAKE YOU LOVE ME ANY LESS. THANK YOU, JESUS.

GOOD SHEPHERD

The Lord is my Shepherd. I will have everything I need.
PSALM 23:1

God is all you need. He will use you to do great things for His glory, but you don't need to chase after things that take your time away from Him. If you spend a lot of time with your friends and a little time with God, then you need to change that.

God will take care of you in the hard times, and He will move things around in your life so you will get rest. God leads you in the right choices. God promises to comfort you when you're sad. No matter what, you do not lack a thing.

Be brave for His glory. Take a minute to thank God for all of His blessings and for holding you. Ask Him to give you opportunities to be a light in your home and school. Be bold and tell people about the Good Shepherd, Jesus, and what He did on the cross. Tell them that God loves them.

THANK YOU FOR TAKING CARE OF ME. I'M SORRY THAT I TAKE YOU FOR GRANTED SOMETIMES. HELP ME TO THINK OF YOU ALWAYS, AND TEACH ME HOW TO FIND ALL MY WORTH IN YOU. PLEASE BLESS MY FAMILY. HELP ME TO SERVE THEM AND BE AN EXAMPLE OF JESUS TO ALL I MEET TODAY.

THE WORD

You have life from God that lasts forever.
PHILIPPIANS 1:28

Your life is a gift from God. As God grows you up as a brave young boy, learn to see each day as a chance to worship Him for everything He's done for you. When you see each day as a chance to make God famous, you will spend less time worrying about the struggles and more time focusing on how big God really is.

What is it that you are worried about? Jesus says over and over that He doesn't want His children worrying. He wants you to have faith that He will calm the storms in your life just as easily as He calmed the storm that was raging around the disciples on the Sea of Galilee. Jesus and His friends were in the same boat, but they got scared. Jesus told the storm to stop, and it obeyed!

Next time you find yourself worrying about something, remember that Jesus speaks and things change. Lift up your fears to Him, and trust that He will calm the storms in your life.

DEAR LORD, THANK YOU FOR THE STORY WHERE YOU CALMED THE RAGING SEAS JUST BY COMMANDING THEM TO STOP. PLEASE SPEAK YOUR PEACE OVER MY LIFE SO I CAN KEEP BEING THE BRAVE BOY YOU CALLED ME TO BE.

WAIT

The LORD always keeps his promises;
he is gracious in all he does.
PSALM 145:13 NLT

God thinks the world of you. Being brave means knowing your true identity is in Jesus. Don't ever feel like you don't matter or you're not as important as other people. That's one of the enemy's lies in your life. He will make you feel unwanted when one of your prayers goes unanswered.

The truth is, God is for you. The unanswered prayers are like God telling you to wait. He has something great in store for you. He needs you to be brave and patient and know that you are complete in Him just as you are.

God doesn't change. That's another lie the devil will tell you to keep you away from feeling loved. He will tell you that God changes daily. God is good, so that means He will be good tomorrow and the next day. God doesn't change the way He feels about you. Wait on Him and be amazed at what He will do through you to bless others.

JESUS, THANK YOU FOR LOVING ME. THANK YOU FOR ALL THE SUFFERING YOU WENT THROUGH ON THE CROSS FOR ME! PLEASE GIVE ME THE COURAGE TO BE PATIENT AND WAIT ON YOU. DON'T LET ME GO!

THANKFUL LIVING

*It was through His loving-kindness that we were born
again to a new life and have a hope that never dies.*
1 PETER 1:3

God loves you so much He sent His only Son, Jesus, to die as a sacrifice to cover all your sins. The God of everything showed you kindness by giving you grace and giving you new life. That is a miracle that you've been given. Let your days be filled with thankful living by telling God how grateful you are for His gift that you could never earn in a hundred lifetimes.

How many instances can you think of where you wished that things worked out differently? Maybe it was a bad grade on a school assignment. Maybe it was a selfish decision that hurt somebody else's feelings. Or maybe it was something you should have done but were too scared to do.

With Jesus there are no regrets. Keep being brave and ask for forgiveness when you mess up, but don't let guilt keep you trapped in the past. You are saved, and you were made to shine for God's glory.

GOD, THANK YOU FOR SETTING ME FREE FROM THE PENALTY THAT I DESERVE. I AM SO THANKFUL THAT I AM FORGIVEN. PLEASE SHOW ME HOW TO DROP ALL MY REGRETS AND LIVE FOR YOU. TEACH ME TO PRACTICE THANKFUL LIVING FOR ALL THAT YOU HAVE DONE FOR ME.

GOOD CHOICES

*Pure religion is also to keep yourself clean
from the sinful things of the world.*
JAMES 1:27

Many distractions in the world tempt you to make bad choices. But God has said in His Word that real religion is all about making good choices. It's not always easy, but pray for God's help as you continue on your journey of brave living.

Making good choices is difficult sometimes. Remember that God is on your side and is with you to help you through hard times. Think about how hard Mary and Joseph had it when they both learned that Mary was pregnant with Jesus! The Bible says that Joseph was really scared and planned to leave Mary. At first he didn't understand what was happening. Then an angel explained the whole thing to them, and they stayed together and made the right choice.

Next time you're faced with a hard decision, go to God and ask Him for help. Then you too will be ready to make the right call.

LORD, DOING THE RIGHT THING CAN BE HARD. PLEASE HELP ME TO OBEY YOU AND MAKE GOOD CHOICES. SHOW ME HOW TO LEARN MORE FROM YOUR WORD EACH DAY SO THAT MAKING THE CORRECT DECISIONS WON'T BE SO DIFFICULT. THANK YOU FOR CARING ABOUT ME.

TESTIFY

Peter replied, "Repent and be baptized, every one of you,
in the name of Jesus Christ for the forgiveness of your sins."
ACTS 2:38 NIV

Some people like to take charge while others like to stay quiet. Some people work hard while others don't do a whole lot. Sometimes people are afraid to do the right thing because they are afraid of failing or afraid that someone will make fun of them.

Jesus' friend Peter was a fisherman before he decided to follow Jesus. But then he started telling people about Jesus. Peter was brave, but he had some up-and-down moments. One time he denied even knowing Jesus because he was afraid of getting arrested. But after Jesus rose to heaven, Peter gave such an amazing testimony that three thousand people became believers!

When it comes to sticking up for Jesus, don't be afraid. God is with you, so keep being brave!

LORD, PLEASE DRAW NEAR AND HELP ME TO KNOW THAT YOU'RE HERE. PLEASE FILL MY HEART. IT'S HARD TO BE BRAVE WHEN I FEEL ALONE. I WISH I COULD SEE YOU, JESUS. I WISH I COULD HUG YOU. I'M SO GLAD TO KNOW THAT ONE DAY I WILL BE ABLE TO!

EXCITED

I am not ashamed of the gospel, because it is the power of God that brings salvation to everyone who believes.
ROMANS 1:16 NIV

Make a list of everything that's important to you. Family? Toys? Books? Friends? Whatever is on your list, make sure that "making God famous" is on it. A very popular man named Paul wrote a lot of the books in the New Testament. He traveled the world to tell as many people as he could that Jesus loved them and died to save them from their sins.

In fact, when Paul was writing his letter to the believers in Rome, he said that he wasn't ashamed of the gospel because it is all-powerful. Do you talk to people about Jesus? If you do, keep it up. If you don't, ask God to give you open doors to share your faith.

Becoming a brave young man means knowing who you stand for. Running after Jesus with everything you have keeps you headed in the right direction. Can you imagine meeting people in heaven one day who are there because you were brave and told them about Jesus?

GOD, I PRAY THAT YOU WOULD HELP ME TO BE BOLD IN SHARING MY FAITH. I WANT TO BE LIKE PAUL AND SHARE THE GOOD NEWS OF JESUS WITH AS MANY PEOPLE AS I CAN. THANK YOU FOR CALLING ME YOUR PRECIOUS CHILD.

MIGHTY WARRIOR

"The LORD your God is with you, the Mighty Warrior who saves."
ZEPHANIAH 3:17 NIV

God is the mighty warrior who fights for you. When you feel like you can't possibly win the struggle you're facing, remember that you are made in His image. You are stronger than you know because God is with you. He saves you from the enemy's attacks and comforts you in the best way possible.

Being brave has its challenges. There are so many distractions, so many things to do. But really, God wants you to simplify things so that your relationship with Him is the main thing you spend your time focusing on. Use your time to read your Bible and listen to the lessons God has for you.

The Bible says that God takes great delight in you. A lot of times, when you feel tired, it's hard to believe that this is true. Be confident, because now that Jesus is your Savior, God's love for you causes Him to sing over you! You are so important to Him!

JESUS, THANK YOU FOR DYING FOR ME. THANK YOU FOR GIVING ME NEW LIFE. I PRAY THAT YOU WILL HELP ME TO BE BRAVER TODAY THAN I WAS YESTERDAY. THANK YOU FOR THINKING THE WORLD OF ME. PLEASE HELP ME TO REMEMBER THAT TRUTH WHENEVER I START TO DOUBT IT.

UNBELIEVABLE

With God's help we will do mighty things.
PSALM 60:12 NLT

King David was very brave. He had a habit of dedicating his military battles to God. He knew that without God's help, he would not be victorious. A lot of the psalms in your Bible were written by David. They were his reflections on the heart and character of God.

David made a ton of mistakes, but he realized he had nothing if he didn't have God. He kept his word, and that was another trait that made David brave. Keep gaining confidence each day as you walk with God and practice keeping your promises. Your parents and teachers will see this and ask where the change came from. That's when you can share how God is molding you into a very brave young boy.

God keeps His promises too. He promises to help you do mighty things. Think about your hobbies and begin thinking about how you can use those to accomplish great deeds for God. You are amazing to Him!

GOD, I KNOW THAT I CAN'T DO ANYTHING OF WORTH WITHOUT YOU. BUT SOMETIMES I FORGET THIS AND TRY TO MAKE THINGS HAPPEN ON MY OWN. REMIND ME WHEN THIS HAPPENS. TELL ME AGAIN AND AGAIN THAT WHEN I TURN MY DAYS OVER TO YOU, THAT'S WHEN YOUR HELP AND POWER BEGIN TO MAKE ME BRAVER THAN EVER.

FORGIVEN

*We have been bought by His blood and made
free. Our sins are forgiven through Him.*
COLOSSIANS 1:14

Have you ever bought something with your own money? It's interesting how we treat things that we paid for. We take care of them. We don't want anyone else to mess with those things. We are proud because we worked hard for them.

That's exactly what Jesus has done for you. He paid for you by His blood that He shed on the cross. That means His blood was the sacrifice needed to cover all your mistakes so that you could have eternal life with Him. Consider this when you think about how much you're worth to Jesus.

How does Jesus treat you? He takes care of you and loves you. He sets you free from all of your guilt so you can spend your days practicing being brave. Jesus doesn't want the devil messing with you, so He protects you from the lies the enemy tries to tell you. Jesus is very proud of you!

JESUS, I WILL NEVER UNDERSTAND EXACTLY WHAT YOU WENT THROUGH FOR ME WHEN YOU CARRIED YOUR CROSS TO THAT LONESOME HILL OUTSIDE OF JERUSALEM. PLEASE FORGIVE ME WHEN I MESS UP. I WANT YOU TO BE PROUD OF ME AS I WORK ON BECOMING A BRAVE BOY. KEEP MY THOUGHTS ON EVERYTHING YOU HAVE DONE FOR ME.

WALLS OF STRENGTH

He is my loving-kindness and my walls of strength,
my strong place and the One Who sets me free.
PSALM 144:2

Brave young boys like you study the traits of God so they will better understand who He is and who they are in Him. If you have a favorite movie, book series, or sports team, you probably have a ton of information about it stored away in your memory bank. Character names. Stats. Funny lines memorized.

Just as you study those things, you'll find that it is even more important to study God. Really get to know Him. For example, God is loving-kindness. He has plans for your life, and since He is a promise keeper, He will fulfill his promises in big ways for you. He is your fortress. Like a castle rising up around you, God is both your protector and your source of power.

God is your strong place. He is the one who sets you free from your struggles. Study these traits and commit them to memory. These are the truths that you can count on both today and tomorrow.

FATHER, I FIND IT TOO EASY TO BE DISTRACTED BY A LOT OF THINGS IN MY LIFE. I PRAY THAT YOU WILL HELP ME TO STUDY MY BIBLE SO I CAN SEE MORE OF WHO YOU ARE AND WHAT IS IMPORTANT TO YOU. I WANT TO BE BRAVE, BUT SOME DAYS IT'S HARD TO CONCENTRATE. THANK YOU FOR BEING PATIENT WITH ME.

NOT AFRAID

You have life from God that lasts forever.
PHILIPPIANS 1:28

You have to trust God. Being brave means remembering what is true. When you feel like God has walked away, do not believe that lie of the enemy. You always matter to God. God doesn't change depending on what situation you're in. The Bible says His love is unfailing, which means His love is constantly filling your heart even when you don't feel it.

The enemy told Adam and Eve that they could disobey God and still get what they wanted. This is the same trick he uses today. After they believed the lie, Adam and Eve immediately felt the guilt that came from their bad decision. Fast-forward. When you make a bad choice, the devil runs in and tells you that God doesn't like you anymore.

But look at how God treated Adam and Eve. The Bible says that after they sinned, Adam and Eve hid from God. And the cool thing is that God went after them! He didn't leave them alone to suffer. Trust that God is fighting for you the same way He covered Adam and Eve.

GOD, I'M SO SORRY THAT I KEEP MESSING UP. PLEASE FORGIVE ME. HELP ME TO REMEMBER THAT YOU ARE ALWAYS FOR ME. HELP ME TO REMEMBER THAT YOU NEVER CHANGE!

GREAT JOY

*"I am the Lord your God Who holds your right hand, and
Who says to you, 'Do not be afraid. I will help you.' "*
ISAIAH 41:13

God is always here to help you. As He grows you into a brave young
boy, keep your heart in the truth. Memorizing Bible verses is a good
way to do this so that God's Word is always with you.

Think of a song you like. You probably have the lyrics memorized, and singing along makes you happy. This is the same when it
comes to reading your Bible. You may be talking with a friend and
discover that they need encouragement. Suddenly you remember
a verse that speaks directly to what they're going through. As you
share the verse, your friend has truth planted in their heart.

Being brave means lifting others up and showing kindness. This
is what God does for you every day, and He's using you to change
your world. He is helping you every step of the way to spread great
joy. He's walking with you. You've got this!

LORD, I WANT TO STUDY YOUR WORD AND COMMIT IT TO MEMORY. I WANT
TO BE PREPARED TO HELP A FRIEND KNOW YOUR PROMISES. HELP ME TO
MEMORIZE VERSES THAT WILL LET ME PLANT SEEDS OF HOPE IN HEARTS.
SHOW ME HOW TO USE MY TIME WISELY. THANK YOU FOR MAKING ME BRAVE.

WITH YOU

*"I have told you these things so you may have peace
in Me. In the world you will have much trouble.
But take hope! I have power over the world!"*
JOHN 16:33

When you think about being brave, you think about doing good things for God and people around you. Another part of being brave is knowing that Jesus is the source of rest. He died to set you free. This is very important. He didn't do all that for you so you would be filled with anxiety; He took up His cross so your heart would be filled with peace.

Jesus told His friends that trouble and bad times lay ahead. But He also told them that He had power over all the bad things in the world. Don't let the bad times get you down. The enemy wants to keep your thoughts on fear, but you have Jesus, so there's nothing to worry about!

The journey to brave living isn't a short one. Think about this new day God has given you in a new way. Let the peace that Jesus has for you change everything.

GOD, I NEED YOU TO HELP ME TO UNDERSTAND THAT YOUR PEACE IS ALWAYS
WITH ME, EVEN WHEN TIMES ARE TOUGH. SHOW ME HOW TO REST IN YOUR
LOVE AND MERCY. THANK YOU FOR WALKING THROUGH LIFE WITH ME.

MAKE A WAY

When I am afraid, I will trust in You.
PSALM 56:3

Brave believers are confident that God is strong enough to help through all of life's good and bad times. Noah lived in a very stressful time, but God used him to be brave and obedient.

In Noah's day, the earth was filled with evil, and God was sad that He had created people. Everyone made bad choices. But God was pleased with Noah and assigned him a project that seemed crazy. God told Noah to build a massive ark. God was going to flood the earth and wipe out everything and everyone except Noah and his family and pairs of all kinds of animals.

The people of Noah's time had never seen rain, so you can imagine how they mocked Noah for building that huge wooden boat on dry land. Still, Noah was brave and obeyed God. When the rains came, Noah, his family, and the animals were safe inside the ark. His obedience and bravery helped his people avoid the disaster of being completely wiped off the earth.

HELP ME TO TRUST YOU, LORD, EVEN WHEN I DON'T UNDERSTAND. HELP ME TO REMEMBER THAT YOU ARE BIGGER THAN ALL OF MY PROBLEMS. THANK YOU FOR NOAH'S EXAMPLE. I PRAY THAT I COULD BE LIKE HIM AND OBEY YOU EVEN WHEN TIMES ARE HARD.

MORE THAN ENOUGH

Be strong. Be strong in heart, all you who hope in the Lord.
PSALM 31:24

God is here and will remind you of His character so your heart can be aligned to His. The more you read about Him in your Bible, the more your heart will be filled with pure joy. You will begin to see Him for who He really is and not who your feelings tell you He should be.

When you lie down at night and when you rise to meet the new day, search your heart and make sure God's truth is the only thing that's planted there. Be silent in front of Him and listen. Hear His merciful voice guide you. Pray for the power of the cross to lead you away from the enemy's lies.

Be brave and make today a day to worship. Let every part of who God made you to be point people back to Him. Let each hour be a beautiful sacrifice of love you offer up to Him while the world watches.

GOD, PLEASE LET MY HANDS GUIDE THE SUFFERING BACK TO YOU. LET MY HANDS CARRY THE WEAK. PLEASE GIVE THEM STRENGTH. KEEP MY EYES FIXED ON HEAVEN SO PEOPLE WILL SEE THAT YOU ARE IMPORTANT TO ME.

HUMBLE

Let us go with complete trust to the throne of God.
We will receive His loving-kindness and have His
loving-favor to help us whenever we need it.
HEBREWS 4:16

Close your eyes and hear God say that He is your Father. He is your King.

He doesn't love only some of your soul. He doesn't care about some of your dreams. He doesn't hold half of your heart in His hands. He created you and made you complete and completely for a relationship with Him. Everything about you matters to Him. The same is true about your prayers. Whether you are asking God for help or lifting up praise, God listens to every word.

From the moment you wake, talk to God. Remember that He was watching over you as you slept. And just as He waits for you to rise in the morning and pray, so He wants you to wait on Him to answer you. But don't wait like one who has no hope. You are His wonderful creation. You are the one He loves and deeply cares for. You mean more to Him than you realize.

THANK YOU FOR LOVING ALL OF ME, GOD. HELP ME TO LIVE TODAY IN CONFIDENCE THAT YOU KNOW MY VOICE. HELP ME TO BE BRAVE, KNOWING THAT YOU ARE ANSWERING ME. THANK YOU FOR FILLING MY HEART WITH HOPE. THANK YOU FOR MY LIFE.

SAFE

There is no fear in love. Perfect love puts fear out of our hearts.
1 JOHN 4:18

Because of God's great love, He has made a way for you to stay safe in His arms. Think about Him and come close, because living your days with Him is how He made you to live. Let your thoughts remain on His commands. Let your words bring Him praise, and let your actions be about bowing down to His holy name.

God has called you His precious child, so you may spend your days thinking about His wonderful love for you. His words to you will be the light that guides you through every situation. Show people how much you care about Him by giving Him all of you.

God sees your heart. He is pleased with you. Strive to be closer to Him. Let your heart beat for all the things that bring Him glory. Be about goodness and righteousness. Have everything to do with the things of God's heart.

JESUS, SHOW ME HOW TO DO EVERYTHING IN LOVE. HELP ME TO STAY HUMBLE. HELP ME TO MAKE THE HARD CHOICES TO STAY AWAY FROM THE THINGS THAT GO AGAINST YOUR WILL. HELP ME TO RUN AWAY FROM THE THINGS YOU DON'T LIKE.

ACT NOW

"You must love the Lord your God with all your heart."
LUKE 10:27

God is here for you. He is here to lead you through every one of the days He has made for you. He goes before you, and He also goes behind to protect your life from the enemy's lies. Use the scriptures to remain on the straight path He has created for you to follow.

God is righteous. He knows that the enemy tries to speak over your heart, and God is proud of you for remembering not to trust any of the enemy's words. They are all lies that go against God's love for you.

The world is full of ugliness. Even though you will encounter people who don't believe what you do, keep your eye on God. He is the only one whose words are trustworthy. The things people in the world run after will bring them down. Keep being brave, and stay away from people who don't want to do what is right.

JESUS, THANK YOU FOR GIVING ME VICTORY OVER MY PROBLEMS. THANK YOU FOR LETTING ME TAKE REFUGE IN YOU. THANK YOU FOR ALWAYS BEING MY SAFE PLACE. SPREAD YOUR ARMS OF PROTECTION OVER ME. YOU ARE AWESOME. HELP ME SHARE THE GOOD NEWS OF JESUS TO THE ONES WHO DON'T BELIEVE IN YOU.

TRUTH

You have faith in Christ because of the power of God.
1 CORINTHIANS 2:5

With Jesus in your heart, you can make each day a song of joy to God. His name is worthy of your love. Rejoice for the new blessings God will bring today. Lift your hands high, and be glad that you are free from the chains of sin. Jesus has brought you home from a place of isolation to the shadow of God's wings.

God surrounds you. His faithfulness is your shield. He spreads His protection over you so that you will never be left open for attack. When God is your refuge, you will be glad. When God is all you want, you will be relieved. With God there are no worries or burdens!

God loves you. The heart of Jesus is the lens through which God sees your life. His heart beats for you. His care for you is so powerful that no wicked act of the evil one can pull you away from Him.

GOD, THANK YOU FOR UNDERSTANDING WHAT I'M GOING THROUGH.
I WANT TO BE BRAVE, AND I'M GLAD YOU ARE WITH ME, BUT SOME DAYS THE
FEELINGS OF GUILT ARE A LOT TO HANDLE. REMIND ME THAT JESUS FREED
ME OF MY GUILT WHEN HE TOOK UP HIS CROSS. THANK YOU, JESUS!

HEROIC

Christic in you brings hope of all the great things to come.
COLOSSIANS 1:27

God's mercy surrounds you and heals you from the things that cause you stress. He knows what it feels like when your heart doesn't feel brave. He knows because He watched Jesus take on the sins of the world. He knows because He saw the soldiers mock His Son and spit on Him. He saw them taunt Jesus with the crown of thorns. He wanted to save Jesus from that darkness, but He also wanted to save you.

When your day is covered with hurt and your body aches and your voice cries out for help, know without doubting that God hears you and is there to help.

Most people don't think about glorifying God, so God doesn't want you to get discouraged when your friends act selfish and hurt your feelings. Most people run after things that make them happy. Don't be tempted by this. Be brave and run after God's love. Go to Him and live.

LORD, PLEASE KEEP YOUR EYES ON ME AND WATCH OVER MY HEART. I KNOW YOU WILL PULL ME THROUGH THE DARK TIMES BECAUSE YOU LOVE ME. YOUR LOVE FOR ME DOESN'T END. MY HEART IS STRONG ENOUGH BECAUSE YOU LOVE ME EVEN ON MY HARDEST DAYS.

RADICAL

Be honored in Your strength, O Lord.
We will sing and praise Your power.
PSALM 21:13

Pain is a heavy burden to bear. It reaches into your soul and keeps you from being brave. Bad days squeeze life from you and wear you out. Instead of worshipping, you groan from the weight of bearing problems you were never meant to carry. But whether the things that bother you are many or few, all of them are temporary. When it seems like your tears become a waterfall of misery, remember that God is here. He will dry your eyes and show you just how amazing your real position as His beloved child really is. Let your faith be renewed by God's love. Keep your eyes on Jesus.

Jesus knows the world is filled with terrible situations that cause sadness. He knows that when you see these things, your heart feels the ache of uncertainty. He knows that sometimes it's hard to be brave. But He wants you to remember that He conquered death. He is on His throne, in His rightful place as your victorious King.

GOD, THE ENEMY HAS TRIED TO FILL MY WORLD WITH SADNESS IN HOPES THAT MY EYES WILL GROW WEAK. HE WANTS ME TO TAKE MY EYES OFF YOU AND KEEP THEM LOOKING DOWN ON THE CRAZINESS IN THE WORLD. HELP ME TO BE BRAVE AND BELIEVE YOUR WORDS. HELP ME TO BE THE EXAMPLE OF HOPE.

AUTHORITY

Wait for the Lord. Be strong. Let your heart
be strong. Yes, wait for the Lord.
PSALM 27:14

In light of everything God has done and is doing for you, spend your hours being thankful. Show gratitude for all the love and hope He gives you by being brave as you live to do His will. Lift up praise for all the blessings He will pour over you. God is faithful and will always keep His word. Let your heart sing. He is your God, the Lord Most High. He is the one who loves you.

Take this new day and consider the holy name of Jesus. Think about how majestic it is in relation to all the things most people consider wonderful. His name is above all other names, and it is grander than anything the enemy tries to sell you. If he entices you with material things, remember the name of Jesus. If he lures you with riches and temporary fixes, remember Jesus. Jesus is here for you to rest in His arms. He is here for you to grow into the brave person He created you to be.

I CAN'T BELIEVE YOU CREATED ME IN YOUR IMAGE, GOD. I PRAY THAT
MY LIFE REFLECTS YOUR HEART FOR PEOPLE. YOU ARE LORD OVER
ALL. PLEASE STIR MY HEART TO WORSHIP YOU ALWAYS.

MAJESTIC

There is strong trust in the fear of the Lord,
and His children will have a safe place.
PROVERBS 14:26

God is your heavenly Father who is worthy of your every desire. Be thankful. Be brave in the way you worship God.

God has made you to be a beacon of hope that points your friends to His loving arms. Live this day by the beat of your grateful heart. Don't be ashamed to tell people about God's great plans for their lives. The enemy wants you to feel like you can't make a difference. He doesn't want you to know that when you worship God with every ounce of your soul, the enemy's plans get defeated.

God has rescued you. He sent Jesus for you. He sits on the throne as the righteous Judge who upholds your life. Part of being brave means remembering that the enemy is a liar who wants you to believe that his power is still effective and that your life really doesn't matter. Being brave, however, means knowing that God's holy name, and not the enemy's lies, is what you live for.

DEAR GOD, I KNOW THAT I CAN ONLY BE BRAVE WITH YOUR HELP AND POWER. I WANT TO TELL ALL MY FRIENDS ABOUT YOU. I WANT TO BE STRONG AND SET A GOOD EXAMPLE FOR THEM. PLEASE HELP ME TO KEEP DOING THIS.

LIVING BOLDLY

*"The Lord is my Helper. I am not afraid
of anything man can do to me."*
HEBREWS 13:6

God is your loving Father who is for you. He is the eternal refuge for you in both good and bad times. He is your stronghold. Being brave is trusting that when He says something, He will follow through. He will never walk away from you. Come after Him. Follow Him, for He will never forsake you or your relationship.

God is worth it all. For every dream you hold close in your heart, God is worth more. For every hurt that burdens your heart, God's love makes a way for you to go on. Be brave and let your life be a song of praise for all that God does. Be bold and tell people about all the blessings He has given you.

Remember, the enemy wants you to keep quiet about Jesus. He wants to lead you to things that will distract you and keep you from the work of sharing the good news of Jesus.

GOD, I KNOW THAT THE ENEMY WANTS ME TO REMAIN SILENT AND RUN AFTER EVERYTHING THAT MAKES ME HAPPY. MOST OF ALL, HE WANTS ME TO FIX MY EYES ON MYSELF. BUT I KNOW THAT YOU DO NOT IGNORE MY PLEAS FOR HELP. SHOW ME HOW TO BE BRAVE TODAY SO THAT YOU GET ALL THE GLORY.

NOT TOO BIG

"If you love Me, you will do what I say."
JOHN 14:15

The silence you experience as you wait on God does not mean that He hasn't heard you, or that He is far away doing something else. The enemy would love for you to believe that God is too big and you are too small to have a close relationship.

Don't find your worth in the devil's lies. Hear God speak with your heart. Feel His mercy when the impossible happens. See Him in the faces of the ones whom Jesus has rescued from their sins. God is here right now to *hold* you and *hear* you and *do* for you. He is your God and your loving Father, and you are His.

In this moment, spend time lifting up praises to Him and let your heart rejoice for the gift of salvation Jesus has given you. Now is the hour to raise your voice in thanksgiving to honor your Savior for defeating the enemy and being your King.

GOD, I KNOW YOU WILL NEVER FORGET ME. WHEN HOPE SEEMS LOST, HELP ME TO REMEMBER THAT YOU ARE HERE TO RESCUE ME. BECAUSE YOU LOVE ME, YOU KEEP ME SAFE AND RESTORE MY HOPE.

DELIVERED

Because of the riches of His shining-greatness, He will make you strong with power in your hearts through the Holy Spirit.
EPHESIANS 3:16

God stands by your side. He is not far away tending to other people. When the enemy tells you that God is far away from you, don't listen. The devil tries to keep your eyes on the stressful parts of life to wear down your spirit.

Not so for God. When trouble arrives, He stands between you and the problems so your eyes will see His glory and goodness. When stress rises up and surrounds you, God will open your eyes so you can help those in need of a Savior find Jesus.

Seek God today. Don't let your pride keep you from following Him to all the blessings He has for you. Be brave and do things God's way. He will show you that His ways are best!

GOD, I KNOW THERE ARE SO MANY PEOPLE WHO NEED TO HEAR ABOUT JESUS. I'M SORRY WHEN I DON'T DO MY QUIET TIME. HELP ME TO MAKE ROOM FOR YOU. HELP ME TO HOLD YOUR COMMANDS CLOSE TO MY HEART AND OBEY THEM. HELP ME TO SEEK YOU IN THE LITTLE THINGS AND TO AVOID PRIDE AND STAY HUMBLE. HELP ME TO LIVE MY LIFE LIKE JESUS.

FEARLESS

"Ask, and what you ask for will be given to you. Look, and what you are looking for you will find. Knock, and the door you are knocking on will be opened to you."
LUKE 11:9

Be brave and don't worry about the things you don't have. Don't worry about things you think you should have. God cares about you and will provide everything you need. Even when it seems like stressful times multiply, God's love for you is greater than all of your bad days combined.

The enemy spins his lies into threats in hopes that you will spend your day worrying about things that are out of your control. Let God carry you. Let God protect you through every storm.

God loves you more than anything. Call out to Him. Tell Him what you need. Think about what Jesus did on the cross. That's being brave!

The people you meet who don't have Jesus in their hearts run and hide from God's grace because they don't understand the free gift of love Jesus gave them on the cross.

LORD, SHOW ME HOW TO SHARE ALL MY THOUGHTS WITH YOU. HELP ME TO LAY ALL OF MY BURDENS AT THE FOOT OF YOUR THRONE. THANK YOU FOR ANSWERING ALL MY PRAYERS!

WINNER

*The prayer from the heart of a man right
with God has much power.*
JAMES 5:16

God is here to take care of you in times of joy and times of sadness. God sees and feels what you're going through. When you're sad, God wants you to know that He takes away the sadness. When you're happy, God is happy for you, so continue to commit your life to Him. He is the one who always helps you.

As you continue working on being brave, know that God disrupts the plans of the wicked so that you will shine like the stars in a dark world. There's nothing the enemy can do to you that will pull you away from God.

Jesus is King of heaven and earth. In Him there is no darkness or trace of sin. In Him there is no shame. He hears your prayers and knows the desires of your heart. Listen to Him encourage you. Be brave and stand tall. Keep shining. God loves you!

THANK YOU, JESUS, FOR DYING FOR ME. YOU ARE MY HOLY LORD. KEEP YOUR WALL OF PROTECTION AROUND MY HEART. THANK YOU FOR CALLING ME YOUR CHILD. PLEASE KEEP GIVING ME COURAGE TO STAND UP FOR WHAT IS IMPORTANT TO YOU. HELP ME TO BE BRAVER TODAY THAN I WAS YESTERDAY.

BIG ADVENTURES

"Do not worry."
MATTHEW 6:31

Trust God to give you the best answers to all of your requests. He always keeps His eyes on you. He always looks ahead to the places you can't see, to make sure you will be safe and shielded. He gives light to your eyes so that you may always find your way through the world's darkness.

God will always protect you from the enemy's traps. Satan will never be able to overcome you, because Jesus is the one who overcame death. Jesus is the one who paid the ultimate price for your heart. He suffered in your place because of love.

Through every situation you face today, trust God and His unfailing love. In times of joy and times of happiness, let your heart rejoice. Praise God for who He is. Let your heart beat for the things that God's heart beats for. Trust Him, even in the hard times.

LORD, THANK YOU FOR TEACHING ME ABOUT TRUST. THANK YOU FOR HOLDING ME THROUGH EVERY SMILE AND EVERY TEAR. EVEN WHEN THE HURTING SEEMS TOO HARD TO BEAR, HELP ME NEVER TO FORGET THAT YOU ARE HOLDING ME AND THAT YOU NEVER LET GO. THANK YOU FOR ALWAYS BEING HERE TO KEEP ME FROM FALLING.

ALL YOU NEED

*Praise the Lord, O my soul. And forget
none of His acts of kindness.*
PSALM 103:2

Being brave means not letting all the questions keep you from moving forward each day. God knows that you have days when your heart cries out for answers. He knows there are moments when you feel like He has forgotten you. Making mistakes even though you try hard can be overwhelming at times, but the effects of what Jesus did for your heart overpower every bad thing.

When the enemy lies and says your prayers go unanswered because God has turned His face from you, you say, "Jesus is my answer. He is all I need!" When the devil tempts you to focus on sorrow, you say, "Today I choose to focus on my Savior!" When it seems like the evil one is winning, you say, "My Lord already won the battle for my heart!"

God is calling you to go into the world and, by the power He has given you, tell the ones who will listen a new story. Tell them what the enemy never does. Tell them that Jesus is the answer!

LORD, I WANT TO TELL PEOPLE THAT JESUS LOVES THEM WITH A LOVE UNLIKE ANY OTHER. HELP ME TO TELL THEM THAT YOU ARE THEIR SAFE PLACE AND WILL PROTECT THEM FROM THE ENEMY'S LIES.

SECOND CHANCES

Then they cried out to the Lord in their trouble.
And He saved them from their suffering.
PSALM 107:13

God made you to live each day with Him. The enemy wants you to feel as if God is in heaven and you are alone on earth. But this is not the truth. God's presence is with you always. Wherever you go, He is there.

Think about this gift today, and let it fill your heart with hope. Walk with God and be brave. Use His strength to live a righteous life. Give to others from the overflow of His love for you. Make hard choices to walk away from sin. Be honest in your relationships.

Think about other people and treat them with respect. Serve them with a full heart and love them like God loves you. Use your words to lift those around you and let them see your Jesus-saved heart. Don't worry about putting up walls to protect your hope. No matter what the world brings your way, nothing can destroy God's love for you.

GOD, HELP ME TO SPEAK KINDNESS EVERYWHERE. HELP ME TO BE LIKE JESUS. LET OTHERS SEE HIS TENDER MERCY IN THE WAY I USE MY WORDS AND THE WAY I TREAT PEOPLE. HELP ME TO SHARE YOUR GRACE WITH THOSE WHO NEED SECOND CHANCES.

MAKE ROOM

*If you say with your mouth that Jesus is Lord,
and believe in your heart that God raised Him from the
dead, you will be saved from the punishment of sin.*

ROMANS 10:9

God loves you. God keeps your life safe. When the enemy lurks around trying to plant lies in your heart, God is there to stop him. When the world wears you down with stress, God is there to hold you in the refuge of His strong arms.

Concentrate on trusting God more today for everything you need. He has given you Jesus. Think about Him all day long. Get to the place where He is all you want because He alone is all you need. He shed His blood to pay the debt you could never pay on your own.

Listen to God teach you about keeping your word. Being brave means being active to make God famous. One way you can do that is by giving your time to help the needy. Give your time to others without expecting anything in return. That's how Jesus lived His earthly life. He gave His time to let other people know they were valuable in God's eyes.

FATHER, I UNDERSTAND THAT THERE WAS ONLY ONE THING I
DESERVED, BUT JESUS SACRIFICED HIMSELF SO I COULD RECEIVE GRACE.
THANK YOU FOR LOVING ME SO MUCH THAT I CAN NOW BE CALLED YOUR
CHILD. HELP ME TO GO TELL OTHERS WHAT YOU'VE DONE FOR ME.

LEADERSHIP

[The Lord] is a safe place in times of trouble.
PSALM 9:9

Being brave means deciding to make Jesus famous. Spend today thinking about Him and all the things He has done for you. Knowing that you are safe in Him, live out this day not wanting anything but to bring glory to the one who took the punishment for your sins on the cross. Treat others in a way that tells Jesus you are grateful for His sacrifice.

The enemy wants people to focus on themselves. He wants people to find happiness in their own selfish pursuits. He wants this so that people might begin to think they don't need a relationship with God. Be brave and let your life show them a difference.

People are watching you love God by the choices you make. They are watching how you lead by giving grace to people who have hurt you. By the power of the Holy Spirit in you, the lost will begin to see that Jesus is the answer.

GOD, I WANT TO BE A BRAVE LEADER. THANK YOU FOR SHOWING ME HOW TO TELL PEOPLE THAT JESUS IS THEIR HOPE AND PROBLEM SOLVER. THANK YOU FOR BEING MY PROVIDER. YOU ARE ENOUGH. I AM SO HAPPY THAT YOU HAVE SAVED ME. THANK YOU FOR LOVING ME.

WORLD CHANGE

Do not worry. Learn to pray about everything.
Give thanks to God as you ask Him for what you need.
PHILIPPIANS 4:6

God has set your life in pleasant places for you to enjoy. He has given you a delightful inheritance. You are safe in His loving arms. The enemy wants you to forge your own path so that you can feel a sense of accomplishment. He always wants you to believe that you are in control and that you should do whatever you want. The enemy does this so that you won't think about praising God. He hopes you will become so preoccupied with chasing your dreams that you will forget to listen to God.

This new day is for you to keep your eyes on God. He is always by your side. Spend your time receiving His grace in every moment. "Grace" means that God gives you something way better than what you deserve. Spend your day rejoicing for all the blessings He has given you. The enemy wants you to let go of grace and run after lies. But it is God's hands that hold you close.

GOD, PLEASE KEEP REMINDING ME THAT YOU ARE NEVER GOING TO ABANDON ME. YOU HAVE ALREADY GIVEN ME ETERNAL LIFE. BECAUSE JESUS SAVED ME, MY HEART IS FILLED WITH JOY. HELP ME TO FOLLOW YOUR TEACHINGS. SHOW ME YOUR PLANS FOR MY LIFE!

LISTEN

Trust in the Lord with all your heart, and do
not trust in your own understanding.
PROVERBS 3:5

God invited a very brave man named Joshua to do big things. Joshua knew a lot about being brave because he was in charge of leading an entire nation. One time Joshua led the Israelites to a city called Jericho. Have you heard of it? It was a massive, intimidating city of stone that rose high up in the air. God called Joshua to lead the army in marching around the city every day for six days. If you're familiar with the story, you know that on the seventh day, they marched around the city seven times with the priests blowing on rams' horns. And on the signal of one long blast, the soldiers were to give a shout. When they obeyed God's instructions, the rock wall imploded and the Israelites captured the city.

Joshua was brave because he listened to God. Marching around the city seemed like a weird idea, but Joshua listened and obeyed. Doing things God's way is always best. That's what brave people do. Think about what God is calling you to do. Step out in faith and watch God do awesome things!

LORD, I WANT TO OBEY YOU. HELP ME TO LISTEN. GIVE ME THE COURAGE TO LIVE MY LIFE THE WAY YOU WANT ME TO LIVE IT. HELP ME TO BE LIKE JOSHUA AND SHOW PEOPLE THAT WHAT YOU SAY IS THE MOST IMPORTANT THING.

DON'T HIDE

The angel of the Lord stays close around those who
fear Him, and He takes them out of trouble.
PSALM 34:7

God always hears your prayers. He always hears your praises and your pleas. Remember, it's the enemy's lie that tells you that God is not personal. It's the enemy's lie that says God doesn't care about you. Be brave, and don't keep anything hidden from Him.

Give everything to God. Part of God's character is honesty. When He says something, it is true. But the enemy speaks from a deceitful heart. His eyes search for wickedness and wrongdoing. Jesus conquered your sin problem. The enemy wants you to forget this and live your days in shame for every mistake you make. This is not why God made you. You were wonderfully made to be with Him.

Spend your day listening for God's voice. Read your Bible and hear Him speak directly to your heart. Let His Spirit guide you and teach you all the lessons He has for you today. Give Him all of you.

GOD, I KNOW THE ENEMY WANTS ME TO BECOME SOMEONE ELSE.
HE WANTS ME TO GET IN THE HABIT OF NOT PRAYING OR READING MY
BIBLE. HELP ME NOT TO BE SELFISH. HELP ME NOT TO BE OKAY WITH SIN.
HELP ME TO BE BRAVE BY BEING HONEST IN MY PRAYERS TO YOU.

EVERYTHING

*Be happy in the Lord. And He will give
you the desires of your heart.*
PSALM 37:4

Through each hour of this new day, commit your time to God. Walk the paths He wants you to walk. God won't let you down. He's not asking you to live a holy life on your own. He gives you His Holy Spirit to live inside you with the same power that raised Jesus from the dead. He will help brave young boys like you to be unselfish.

The enemy wants you to worry about doing everything you want. That's not what God wants for you. He made you to let Him be your everything. Let His great love for you be your daily treasure.

Also, don't look to the world for answers. A lot of people you will meet don't have a relationship with Jesus, so they won't have the same goals you have. Don't be discouraged when they say things that you don't agree with. Make a choice to do what is right even if everyone around you is doing the wrong thing.

GOD, THANK YOU FOR SHOWING ME HOW TO BE BRAVE. AS I GROW, I'M SEEING THE TRUTH THAT YOU ARE EVERYTHING I NEED. I'M UNDERSTANDING THAT THE DEVIL WILL TELL ME TO TAKE CARE OF MYSELF, WHEN THE TRUTH IS THAT YOU MADE ME TO BE LOVED BY YOU. THANK YOU, GOD, FOR MEETING ALL MY NEEDS.

INTEGRITY

"Call on Me in the day of trouble. I will take you out of trouble, and you will honor Me."
PSALM 50:15

Be the one who stands up for God. Show others what His name really means by the way you show them Jesus. Speak truth and let your praises to God be the key that unlocks hardened hearts. Serve the lost with kindness so that they might put down their pride and run after Jesus.

This is exactly what a man named Ananias did. God called Him to do a very awkward thing, but Ananias loved God and was very brave and obeyed God.

God had called Ananias to meet Paul and help him see again. Remember, Paul had gone by the name of Saul and was wicked to people who followed Jesus. At the time, Saul didn't know Jesus and made many bad choices. That's when God knocked him to the ground and made him go blind. Ananias didn't want to help someone who had been hurting the people Jesus loved.

But God told Ananias that it was okay because Saul, now Paul, had fallen in love with Jesus. Finally, Ananias wanted to obey God. He went and helped Paul.

LORD, HELP ME TO HAVE INTEGRITY. GIVE ME THE COURAGE TO DO
WHAT YOU WANT ME TO DO, EVEN IF IT SEEMS CRAZY.

GOD, OUR STRENGTH AND COMFORT

You are rich in loving-kindness to all who call to You.
PSALM 86:5

Becoming brave is becoming satisfied with the promises God gives you. Find Him in the hours of waiting and the hours of rejoicing. Know that while you are living your life for Him, He is protecting you.

If you feel sad, God rises up and brings you joy. When you feel worn down, know that He is right there with outstretched hands, waiting to save you from the storms. When you are exhausted and feel powerless to take another step, God is there to carry you.

The gift of life God has given you is just that: a gift. You don't have to use each one of your days trying to earn His love. He is there to be your everything. God is your strength, which means you don't have to try to be strong. God is your rock, so you don't have to try to do things in fear. You are wonderfully taken care of by the powerful God of the universe!

GOD, WHEN STRESS COMES, REMIND ME THAT I AM ANCHORED TO YOU. I AM GRATEFUL THAT NOTHING WILL MOVE YOU AWAY FROM ME. I'M GLAD I DON'T HAVE TO PRETEND THAT THINGS ARE OKAY WHEN THEY'RE NOT. THANK YOU FOR HOLDING ON TO ME.

GOD'S PRECIOUS CHILD

I will sing to the Lord, because He has been good to me.
PSALM 13:6

Be brave and decide every day that you want your life to keep making God famous. He doesn't judge your acts of worship, looking for just the right response. The enemy wants you to feel like you will never be good enough. He hopes you will always feel unworthy of God's favor. He wants your mistakes to be your undoing. Most of all, the enemy wants you to completely forget about Jesus. All God has to do is look at you to receive praise, because Jesus has made you into a new creation! The new life He gave you radiates grace. You are so special to God.

God knows exactly what you need. Keep being brave, because God is not far away, occupied with jobs that take His eyes off you. All day, in every moment, God is with you.

When the arms of sin reach out to attack your hope, God is there to hold them back. When the hands of hurting try to grab your heart, He is there to stop them. Be confident that you are God's precious child.

WHEN I FEEL ALONE AND SCARED, PLEASE REMIND ME THAT I MATTER TO YOU. THANK YOU FOR ALWAYS LOVING ME, JESUS.

NEVER SEPARATED

He has taken our sins from us as far as the east is from the west.
PSALM 103:12

Today, think about God. He gave you a very special gift. He gave you Jesus! Spend time thinking about the depth of God's love for you and the lengths He went to save your soul. Remember that God reached out and took hold of you and pulled you out of the deep waters of sin. When hard times come, remember His words. God thought so much about you that when you were drowning in the darkness of your sins, He first pursued you. When you were lost and had no idea that He made you special, His love parted the skies and came down for you. When you were running away from the truth, His grace caught you and finally set you free.

God pushed the darkness away from you and opened up your eyes. He didn't get mad at you or show you His wrath. He gave you His love and showed you Jesus. From one end of the earth to the other is how far away God removed your sin problem from where you and I stand today.

FATHER, I KNOW I WILL STILL MAKE A LOT OF MISTAKES. THANK YOU FOR REMINDING ME THAT THEY CAN NEVER UNDO YOUR LOVE FOR ME. I'M SO THANKFUL THAT MY SINS CAN NEVER REMOVE YOUR HANDS FROM HOLDING ME.

WORTHY BY FORGIVENESS

"Be sorry for your sins and turn from them."
REVELATION 3:3

God made you, and He doesn't want you to be sad. He delights in you and wants to watch you enjoy today. He wants you to understand that you have been saved and have been given a new freedom in Him.

With Jesus as your Shepherd, you have been relocated to a spacious pasture of favor. The enemy wants you to believe that nothing God says is true. The enemy whispers lies and hopes that you will feel defeated despite the victory for your heart that Jesus won on the cross.

Rest in God's peace. Live free by the power of His grace. Ignore the enemy's lies. Follow God and do what He says. Just as He doesn't turn away from you, remain with Him. You stand blameless before Him, so don't let the evil one say you belong in the dark. You have been cleansed by your Savior, so don't listen to the enemy say your current mistakes make you unworthy of God's love.

GOD, I KNOW THERE IS NOTHING IN THE WORLD THAT CAN CHANGE WHO YOU ARE. I DON'T WANT TO WASTE A SECOND BELIEVING THAT I AM ANYTHING LESS THAN WHO YOU SAY I AM. I AM YOUR CHILD. THANK YOU FOR FORGIVING ME AND HELPING ME TO BE BRAVE.

ALWAYS RETURNING TO GOD

Return to the Lord your God, for He is full of loving-kindness.
JOEL 2:13

God is faithful. He will never let you down. He listens to your prayers. He is your refuge and support. He never goes back on His Word; He keeps all His promises. And today you can be more like Him as you grow in bravery and faithfulness.

Let your faith grow by spending more time with God. Read His words more and listen to Him more today than you did yesterday. Learn more about His character from your Bible and consider how good He really is. He will always be the one who cares about everything you're going through. God loves you.

God doesn't change. He won't love you today and forget about you tomorrow. There is no fault in God. His mighty name is holy. When you open your Bible, you will find that God is a Father who never abandons His children. You'll read that He sent His only Son to bear a criminal's cross for you. Let these truths be the strength you need to keep getting braver and braver.

GOD, I AM SO GLAD YOU CARE ABOUT ME. THANK YOU FOR ALWAYS WATCHING OVER ME AND LEADING ME. HELP ME TO SPEND MORE AND MORE TIME WITH YOU EACH DAY.

GOOD FATHER

"Do not be afraid of them or of what they say."
EZEKIEL 2:6

The world has so many distractions. If you don't concentrate on being brave, it will be easy for you to forget how much you mean to God. He wants you to know you are eternally forgiven. He is your loving Father. Rejoice in the truth that He chose to rescue you! Worship Him with a thankful heart and feel Him hold you close.

God wants you to see today as an opportunity to move closer to Him and further away from the world. Open your Bible and find out more about His character. Find out more of who He is and how much He cares about your life. He knows there are times when temptations feel too strong to resist. He knows that sometimes it feels like the bad days won't end.

God will always make a way to save you. Keep your eyes on His promises. God is here to turn all your darkness into light.

GOD, PLEASE LOOK OUT FOR ME. THANK YOU FOR PROTECTING MY HEART FROM THE ENEMY'S TRICKS. PLEASE LET YOUR LOVE KEEP ME HUMBLE. WITH YOU, I WILL DO ALL THE THINGS YOU HAVE PLANNED FOR ME TO DO!

SHEPHERD

Follow what is good.
3 JOHN 1:11

God is perfect, and His plans for you are nothing less. He gives you His word that He'll never leave you or turn His back on you. He gives you promises to increase your faith and to remind you that you have a hope and shield to counteract the enemy's lies.

Continue to find your refuge in God. The world has many things that compete for your affection. Don't bow down to any of them. God is the one true God. He is your good Shepherd, keeping your path secure. The enemy is powerless against Him.

God is the glorious one who forges a clear path for you to reach high places for His kingdom purposes. This is why He needs you to be brave. Take the moments when it seems like nothing is happening and listen for His voice to call you and lead you on. Listen to Him and learn from His words. Your Bible is truth, and with it He is training your hands and mind for the battle of bravery.

GOD, HELP ME TO USE MY BIBLE SO I CAN LEARN TO FOLLOW YOUR SHEPHERDING MORE CLOSELY. MAKE ME A BRAVE WITNESS FOR JESUS! IN HIS GREAT AND MIGHTY NAME, I PRAY.

THE LORD HEARS HIS CHILDREN

"Whoever receives one of these little children in My name, receives Me."
MARK 9:37

God will never stop loving you. He won't bless you today and take your blessing away tomorrow. The enemy will surely tell you that time spent with God is merely rules and requirements. Jesus died for you to be free from your old life. He destroyed your enemy and crushed his plan to pull you away.

Be brave and follow God to a deeper understanding of who He is and who you are in Him. Let His love grow inside of you and help you realize how much God loves you.

The enemy doesn't care when you feel sad. The world is not listening to you. Neither the world nor the devil will answer your prayers. Both are concerned with other things, and your life is meaningless to them. This is not so with God.

God hears every word you speak and considers each one. When you feel down, it is His strength that lifts you up to see hope rising with the sun. It is His love for you that takes your pleas and turns them into answered prayers.

GOD, THANK YOU FOR HEARING ALL MY PRAYERS AND CARING ABOUT ME. THANK YOU FOR REMINDING ME THAT I AM IMPORTANT TO YOU. LET YOUR HOPE AND LOVE BLOOM IN ME FOREVER.

YOU BELONG TO THE KING!

Do not be proud.
ROMANS 11:20

Remember that today is another day for you to experience God's protection as He delivers you from the enemy's attacks. Today is another gift of blessing for you to receive and cherish. Let God lead you to people who will listen to your testimony. They will see a difference in you and begin to wonder about Him. They will see Jesus in you and begin to lose their desire to run after worldly treasure. People will start to wonder about the kind of love that rescued you from the chains of sin. Some will even draw close and give their lives to God. You have God's kingdom-changing power. Your life matters.

Shout to the world that God is alive. Let your actions remind people that He is your rock. Let them hear you praise God for sending you Jesus. They will know that God is your protector. They will see how He guards your heart from the devil's lies. They will see how He saves you daily from the effects of sin.

FATHER, I AM SO GLAD YOU CALL ME YOUR CHILD. LET YOUR UNFAILING
LOVE FILL MY HEART TODAY. LET YOUR GRACE COVER ME AND
YOUR MERCY GIVE ME THE COURAGE I NEED TO BE BRAVE.

ALL CREATION

Jesus helped His followers understand everything when He was alone with them.
MARK 4:34

Don't be discouraged. Don't lose heart. God is here for you, and He will never abandon you. Look up and see creation declare God's glory. The heavens reflect His goodness. The skies reflect His grace. Everything He made bears His love. Every star. Every sunset. Every ocean and every mountain. All of these speak of God's heart's desire to create wonderful things. You are worth more to Him than all of these combined.

Let your life, perfectly saved by Jesus and hidden in Him, be brave and show others His love. Let your days and nights be filled with praises for all He has done.

The enemy sees you working hard to be brave. He tries to find ways to get in the way of your love for God. But don't lose heart, for the Holy Spirit is your guardian who fights for you. Just as the mountains, which have no voice, still speak of God's glory, so does your life.

LORD, I KNOW THAT YOUR CREATION IS WITNESSED IN ALL THE EARTH. I PRAY THAT THE WORK OF MY HANDS WILL BE ENOUGH OF A VOICE TO REACH THROUGH THE NOISE AND GIVE PEOPLE A PICTURE OF YOUR MERCY AND GRACE.

HAVE MERCY

"Learn to do good. Look for what is right and fair."
Isaiah 1:17

Being brave means seeing your Bible as more than letters on a page or stories written so long ago that their meanings have been diluted by time. God wants you to cherish His words. They are worth more than gold because they are eternal. By reading the words of scripture, your eyes are open to the enemy's schemes. Satan is a strong foe who tries to distract you and persuade you to keep your Bible closed.

By meditating on God's decrees, you will discover great rewards of mercy and grace. Your heart isn't convicted of sin on its own. It's God's truth that opens your heart and leads you away from sin. It's God's righteous words that carry you.

Let God's words keep you from pursuing worldly things. Let them help you focus your eyes on Jesus so that sin has no influence over you today. Jesus is your King. He rules over your heart. He is the one who made you blameless in God's eyes!

THANK YOU FOR REMOVING THE STAIN OF SIN FROM MY LIFE, JESUS. THANK YOU FOR WASHING MY HEART AND MAKING IT NEW. YOU ARE MY ROCK. YOU ARE MY SAFE PLACE AND MY SALVATION. YOU ARE MY HOPE AND EVERYTHING I NEED.

ENCOURAGEMENT

*"The one who loves Me will obey My
teaching. My Father will love him."*
JOHN 14:23

Keep being brave, because God's love for you is active. It seeks you out no matter where you are or what situation you are in and reminds you that everything is going to be okay. God's heart celebrates you and is eager to go before you today to lead the way. Like the sun, His love for you rises in the morning and covers you all day long. No part of today will be outside of His love for you. His words are perfect, and they are here to renew your soul.

The directions God has to offer you are right. Everything He says is meant to bring joy to your heart. Whether you are reading words about His character or things He has done to help His children, it's all for your benefit. He speaks words of radiance to give light to your eyes so you will be able to walk through the world's dark paths. The promises He has for you are unshakable. He has ordained all your days!

LORD, I KNOW YOU KNOW WHAT LIES AHEAD. HELP ME TO SPEND THIS NEW DAY FALLING INTO A DEEPER LOVE OF YOUR WORD. I PRAY THAT YOU WILL USE THIS DAY TO GROW IN ME A HOLY FEAR OF YOUR PURE HEART.

EMPTY HANDS

*For Ezra had set his heart to learn the Law of the
Lord, to live by it, and to teach His Laws in Israel.*
EZRA 7:10

God will answer you. He will even do more than you ask because
He loves you. His name is mighty enough to protect you. Helping
you feel His presence in life's storms is one of the ways He shows
His love. Keeping His hands under you to support you is another.
He holds all of your days that He has ordained for you. The enemy
wants you to believe that you have no Creator and you are on your
own. He hopes that you will invite sin and darkness into your heart
and believe there are no consequences. The enemy wants you to
believe you can be okay without God.

One of the ways you can be reminded of God's presence is
through sacrifice. When you make giving a priority, you open up
room in your heart for God to enter in. When you let go of the world's
treasure, He is able to fill your empty hands with more of His grace.

JESUS, YOU ARE THE ONE WHO IS WORTHY OF ALL MY PRAISE. HELP ME
TO GIVE UP THE DESIRE FOR WORLDLY THINGS. HELP ME TO PUT DOWN
SELFISHNESS AND PRIDE AND FREE UP MY HANDS TO HOLD ON TO YOU!

DESIRE KINGDOM PLANS

I will remember the things the Lord has done.
PSALM 77:11

Let the desire of your heart be a strong relationship with God. Give Him all of your plans and desires. Live each of your days with a joyful heart for the victory that He has given you in Jesus. Let your life be a banner that tells the enemy and the world that God is the most important thing in your life. God is listening to everything you are asking Him to do.

Listen to God's voice speak over you. Pay attention to His words, and let them echo through this new day. God is reminding you of who you really are in Him and not who the enemy says you are. God has anointed you. He has called you His own. You have been redeemed by the blood of the Lamb. Your sins have been forgiven, and your inheritance in the Father's kingdom is secure. You have nothing to worry about or fear because God is with you all of your days.

GOD, PLEASE SHAPE ME TODAY FOR YOU. GO BEFORE ME TO MAKE MY PATH STRAIGHT. NO MATTER WHAT WORLDLY DESIRES AND PLANS TEMPT ME, I KNOW I WILL BE VICTORIOUS WHEN I GO ABOUT DOING THE WORK YOU ARE CALLING ME TO FOR YOUR KINGDOM.

GOOD THINGS

"You planned to do a bad thing to me.
But God planned it for good."
GENESIS 50:20

God is here with answers. He is here to help you understand what you mean to Him. He is always with you. He won't leave you alone for even a small part of this day. He is giving you power to take your eyes off the world and put them on His words. He is giving you strength to stop trying to make things go the way you think they should and let Him take control of every part of your life. Use your blessings to do His kingdom work. Let your life rise above the fray and stand firm on His promises.

Trust God. He knows there are days when this is very hard for you to do. You look around and see people trusting in products of their own design that they believe will protect them. They will trust in other people too. They will listen to teachings that don't have their roots in God. The enemy is leading many astray, and he wants you to follow because, in the end, even he knows that those who don't have Jesus as their Savior will fall.

GOD, I WANT TO MAKE MY LIFE COUNT. HELP ME SIMPLY TO TRUST YOU!

BLESSINGS OF MERCY

The faithful love of the LORD never ends!
His mercies never cease. Great is his faithfulness;
his mercies begin afresh each morning.
LAMENTATIONS 3:22–23 NLT

Spend time thinking about how God's faithful love helps you. Let His power in you bring you joy as you realize its benefits. God's strength and love carry you, not only when you're weak, but even on your brightest days. They take you over life's pitfalls to keep you focused on His protection. His loving strength conquered the enemy's desire to see you wither in your sins.

God's strength makes a way for you to stand up for righteousness and proclaim His glory. Don't listen to the enemy when he lies about your ability to get things done. You are a mighty saint, useful and very important.

Each morning God wants you to feel Him greet you with new blessings of mercy. See Him present you new truths as you read your Bible and find more of His character on its pages. He knows what your heart longs for, and He is not holding back His grace in honoring your requests. He is here for you. He will shower you in new mercies today.

JESUS, THANK YOU FOR YOUR LOVING MERCY TOWARD ME.
STRENGTHEN ME TO STAND UP FOR RIGHTEOUSNESS IN YOUR NAME.

SEND ME

Then I heard the voice of the Lord, saying, "Whom should I send? Who will go for Us?" Then I said, "Here am I. Send me!"
ISAIAH 6:8

Take this new day and turn the hours into praise. Let your words and actions be a worship song sung back to God, for He is worthy. Be brave and practice doing for others what He is doing for you. You are more capable than you know because you have God's power to do all these things and more. Praise Him today by caring for a friend who is sad and broken. Tell him how much Jesus loves him. Tell him that God sees him and knows his name. Pray for your friend.

God is holding you and never letting go! His heart is for you to feel a special love that lets you know how much your life means. Today He wants to remind you of His power and protection. He knows how easy it is for you to grow weary. Even though the day presents you with constant activities and tasks that drain you, He is walking by your side to help you.

GOD, PLEASE SEND ME TO HELP MORE PEOPLE KNOW YOU. I PRAY THAT YOUR HANDS HOLD BACK ALL THE THINGS THAT WILL TRY AND GET IN MY WAY. THANK YOU FOR PLANTING JOY IN MY HEART. HELP ME TO KEEP BEING BRAVE FOR YOUR GREAT NAME'S SAKE.

HE UNDERSTANDS LIKE NO ONE ELSE

[The Lord] will again have compassion on us.
MICAH 7:19 NIV

God understands. As soon as you feel connected to God and His promises, the enemy strikes hard. He hears you thank God for a blessing and immediately sends a conflict. Just as soon as you feel God's love fill your heart, the devil is there to try and steal your joy. His deception is strong, but fear not, for God is stronger. God is bigger. God is wiser. God is better. God is kinder. So much so that He allowed His only Son to be poured out as an offering for you. He allowed His heart to be broken for your sake so you could have the chance to call out to Him and be saved.

God understands there are times when you both share a beautiful moment, and then it seems as if the enemy drains you of all hope. Just when you use God's strength to move a mountain, it seems as if the enemy causes another one to crumble over you. Just when you feel God's arms surround you, the devil threatens to steal your peace. But God is bigger. He keeps you safe in His arms!

THANK YOU, JESUS, FOR THINKING ABOUT ME AND UNDERSTANDING WHAT
I GO THROUGH. THANK YOU FOR TAKING UP YOUR CROSS FOR ME.

ASK GOD

For the Lord God helps Me.
ISAIAH 50:7

The enemy can try all he wants to confuse you, but the simple truth is that God loves you and understands what burdens you. He will always tell you what is right. Keep your Bible open and rely on Him to lead you every day. Let His words strengthen your soul. Believe God when He says the devil is powerless to take you away from Him. Cry out to God, for He is listening. Allow Jesus to take over daily. Live all this new day for your King!

God is for you all day long. The enemy works hard to make you believe that God is gone. But the truth is that God has been with you since the moment He formed you in your mother's womb. God is giving you the strength you need to complete the tasks He is calling you to do. He promises to help you every time you pray. He will always deliver you from the power of darkness. Always be brave, for God is always on your side.

LORD, I DON'T WANT TO LET THINGS THAT ARE OUT OF MY CONTROL BOTHER ME. PLEASE CONTINUE TO TEACH ME HOW IMPORTANT BEING BRAVE IS. SHOW ME HOW TO GLORIFY YOU MORE TODAY THAN I DID YESTERDAY.

THE LIONS' DEN

"May your God, Whom you are faithful to serve, save you."
DANIEL 6:16

Sometimes God seems silent. You've prayed a million times for a specific thing and nothing changes. No matter what you're going through, be brave and don't quit. Don't give up on God. Keep praying a million times more. God isn't quiet because He wants to punish you.

God loved Daniel very much. Yet Daniel found himself in an extremely stressful situation. King Darius had a rule that all the people in his kingdom would bow and worship only him. Of course, Daniel couldn't obey this rule, for he only worshipped God. In fact, he knelt down and prayed to God three times a day.

The king found out about Daniel disobeying his rule and had Daniel thrown into the lions' den. Talk about scary! The next day, the king went to check on Daniel, and Daniel was alive! He told the king that God had sent an angel to shut the mouths of the lions.

LORD, HELP ME TO BE LIKE DANIEL. HELP ME TO BE BRAVE AND TRUST YOU EVEN WHEN I CAN'T HEAR YOU. I PRAISE YOU FOR SAVING ME. THANK YOU, JESUS!

YOUR FORTRESS

"He is without blame, a man who is right and good.
He fears God and turns away from sin."

JOB 2:3

You are filled with God's Spirit who opens your eyes to more of His truth. His Spirit will give you the words you need to spread God's glory to others. Focus on this part of your calling so that your heart will be rooted in God.

God is not far away from you. When God says that He is your fortress, He means that He is surrounding you with His protection and filling you with His strength so that you can do mighty things. The enemy wants you to believe that this is a lie. He wants you to go through each day feeling powerless to do anything. He hopes you will accept the daily routines as all there is in life, because he's afraid of your potential when you rely on God.

Don't live frustrated. Don't let the enemy get a grip on your thoughts by telling you that God is never going to answer certain prayers. Everything about you matters to God. He does not hide His face from you when you pray. He wants to shower you with grace all the time, and He carries you through every moment of every day.

GOD, REMIND ME NOT TO BE AFRAID. I KNOW YOU WILL ANSWER EVERY
PRAYER. WHILE I WAIT, LET MY HEART BE FILLED WITH YOUR LOVE.

CRYING OUT TO GOD

God will never forget the needy;
the hope of the afflicted will never perish.
PSALM 9:18 NIV

The enemy would love for you to get caught up in the stresses of life so that you only focus on your problems. He does this so you will become discouraged and forget to cry out for God's help.

Turn to God. That small step alone brings Him glory. When you keep your eyes on God, you will see His strength. You will be able to see how He holds your life in His hands. Turn to Him and let your heart see that He really is on His throne. The enemy lies to you and says that God has gone away. The truth is that He has your life safe in His arms. And that's where it will always be.

Hear God's voice shake the desert places of loneliness and twist up the mighty oaks of excuses that stand to stop you from following God. Listen for Him, even on the loudest days when the world's noises make it hard to hear.

LORD, PLEASE HELP ME LISTEN TO YOU. I KNOW YOUR VOICE IS POWERFUL. THANK YOU FOR LOVING ME AND MAKING ME BRAVE. LET ME NEVER FORGET TO CRY OUT TO YOU IN MY TIME OF NEED.

REST IN GOD

Yes, my soul, find rest in God; my hope comes from him.
PSALM 62:5 NIV

Today is about simply resting in God. Even though you have school and other everyday responsibilities, He wants you to learn more about Him. Don't get distracted by looking ahead and trying to control your future. Don't waste today by worrying about tomorrow. Slow down and walk with God. His favor is on you. He knows that there are many sorrowful things that try to take your focus off being brave. But those can never take away your hope. Tears from sadness only last a little while, but rejoicing in the truth that God loves you lasts a lifetime. He has made your heart secure. No plan or temptation from the enemy can shake you.

Be brave and make today all about resting in Jesus. Continue to consider everything He has done for you. Praise Him with all your heart. God hears all your prayers, and He always grants you mercy. Make Him your help.

GOD, PLEASE KEEP LEADING ME ON OUR WALK TOGETHER THROUGH THIS LIFE. YOU ARE MY REST WHEN THE PATH IS TOUGH. PLEASE FORGIVE MY MISTAKES AND CLOTHE ME WITH GRACE. THANK YOU FOR SETTING ME FREE. LET MY SOUL PRAISE YOU ALL DAY LONG.

IN CONTROL

*" 'Not by strength nor by power,
but by My Spirit,' says the Lord of All."*
ZECHARIAH 4:6

Commit everything you do to God. Don't hold on to anything. Give every expectation for today to Him and watch God bless you with more than you could ever wish or hope for. Let Him be the one who delivers you out of every trial. Let Him continue to show you how faithful He is. Don't try finding answers in material things. Don't try finding answers in other people. Trust in God. Cling to Him. Be content to wait on Him by remaining in the glow of His love for you. He knows and understands all your burdens. He wipes away the tears when your soul feels anguish, and He smiles when your heart is happy.

Find all your worth in God. Seek Him and know that He is giving you rest in wide-open places. Be brave by not worrying or fearing anything. God is in control, and He loves you. Even when the days find you weak and tired, He gives you strength.

LORD, I KNOW THAT EVERY DAY ISN'T GOING TO BE PERFECT. WHEN GRIEF COMES AND MEETS ME, PLEASE SHOW ME GRACE. I DON'T WANT TO SETTLE FOR ANYTHING ELSE THAN YOU. FILL MY HEART AND REMIND ME OF HOW SPECIAL I AM TO YOU.

LIFE

"My sheep hear My voice and I know them. They follow Me."
JOHN 10:27

Brave boys like you know that God has a storehouse of blessings. Find your shelter in Him alone and receive protection in His presence. Your life is safe in God. He will help you to keep your eyes on Him rather than being distracted by the things of the world.

Sometimes people might hurt your feelings, but don't let that get you down. They don't tell of your worth in God. Other people don't have the final say about how much you mean to God. He is always there to build you up and speak loving words over you. His compassion for you is abundant. God lifted your life out of the darkness so people can see how brave you are. God is making you into a leader.

God has great things planned for your life. Remember, you are not a mistake, so trust that He knows what you need. He hears your prayers. See how much He loves you. Rest in Him. Keep your hope in His promises. Don't let the enemy lie his way into your thoughts. Don't let him tell you that God is far away.

GOD, THANK YOU FOR BEING HERE WITH ME. PLEASE KEEP MAKING ME STRONG. I WANT TO BE FAITHFUL TO YOU. PLEASE KEEP FILLING MY HEART UP WITH YOUR MERCY SO I CAN GIVE IT AWAY TO OTHERS.

COURAGEOUS FOR GOD

*Put on all of God's armor so that you will be able to
stand firm against all strategies of the devil.*
EPHESIANS 6:11 NLT

Being brave can happen in a lot of different ways. A long time ago, a very brave woman named Esther went from living a quiet life to becoming a queen. But along the way, Esther had to make some hard decisions. She wanted to honor God, so she did the hard things it took to do that.

The king chose Esther to be queen. Esther did not tell him that she was Jewish. The king had a friend named Haman who wanted to hurt the Jewish people. Esther had to go to the king and stop the evil plan. At the time, there was a rule that said if any person went to talk to the king without being invited, that person would be put to death! But Esther had faith that God was on her side, so she bravely went to the king and told him about Haman's plan. Because of her actions, the Jewish people were saved.

Think about how you might be able to honor God by sticking up for what is right. You can always count on God's holy armor to protect you.

LORD, THANK YOU FOR THE STORY OF ESTHER. I WANT TO BE THAT BRAVE TOO!
HELP ME TO BE COURAGEOUS AND STAND UP FOR PEOPLE WHO NEED HELP.

BRAVE AND BLESSED

Show me loving-kindness, O God, show me loving-kindness.
PSALM 57:1

God is holding you. All the hours of this new day are in His hands. Trust Him when He says you have nothing to fear. It's okay to wonder, but don't worry. He is your God. He is here to deliver you from the enemy's lies. God keeps His face shining over you, and He continues to save you from uncertainty by His unfailing love.

God knows that you have prayed prayers that seem to have gone unanswered. He knows you still have dreams that have gone unfulfilled. He loves you, and He promises that today is for you to continue calling out to Him. He will not let you fail. He has not forgotten you. Today, know that He hears you and cares about you. Concentrate on what He has done for you. Wait on Him patiently.

You are brave and blessed because you are forgiven. You are brave and blessed because Jesus covered all your sins. You are brave and blessed because of what Jesus has done for you. Your mistakes are no longer a problem, for they don't keep you and Jesus apart from each other.

THANK YOU, JESUS, FOR LOVING ME. HELP ME TO BE STRONG
TODAY. I PRAY THIS IN YOUR AWESOME NAME.

SING

*"Choose from the people able men who fear God,
men of truth who hate to get things by doing wrong."*
EXODUS 18:21

The enemy wants you to believe that keeping quiet is best. He has told you to live your life in silence. He wants you to feel like you have been left alone to carry your own burdens. The truth is that God has made you to sing His praises. He has made you to be not only the hands and feet of Jesus but also His voice. Call out to the lost and hurting. Boldly proclaim your Savior's sweet and holy name.

The enemy wants you to waste time. He wants you to worry about how much you can do on your own. He doesn't want you to trust God to work things out. He doesn't want you to abide in God. He is satisfied when you try solving problems you weren't made to solve. He wants you to find value in holding on to control. He wants you to believe his lies that you are self-sufficient. He doesn't want you to see sin as a problem.

God, however, wants you to follow Him—forever!

HELP ME TO BE OPEN AND HONEST WITH YOU, GOD. HELP ME TO BE BRAVE BY CONFESSING ALL MY SINS. HELP ME TO REMAIN FAITHFUL TO YOUR WILL FOR MY LIFE. SURROUND ME WITH YOUR LOVE, AND PROTECT ME.

WORSHIP THE KING

"If anyone serves Me, My Father will honor him."
JOHN 12:26

Jesus said that if you really want to serve Him, you have to follow Him. He went on to say that those who serve Him will be honored by God. Being brave is making what is important to Jesus important to you. Jesus cared about other people. He wanted them to know they mattered.

Jesus used the phrase "lose your life" to describe what following Him looks like. Make all your time count for Him. Instead of being selfish, think about all the people in your family. How can you use your time to treat them like Jesus would? Think about how you can serve your family and show them the love of Jesus.

Jesus didn't wait for someone else to do the hard work. He did what had to be done to help others. Be brave and decide today to follow Jesus by reading your Bible and discovering how He treated people. Serve Him by loving others and reminding them that Jesus loves them more than anything.

LORD, IT'S HARD TO STOP DOING WHAT I WANT ALL THE TIME. SHOW ME HOW TO USE MY TIME TO HELP MY FAMILY AND OTHERS. MOST OF ALL, I WANT TO SERVE YOU, JESUS. I WANT TO LIVE MY LIFE TO BRING YOU GLORY.

DON'T TURN AWAY

"Then you will call, and the Lord will answer.
You will cry, and He will say, 'Here I am.' "
ISAIAH 58:9

God created the heavens and all of the heavenly bodies by speaking them into existence. And still today He keeps them all moving in their proper orbits. Yet He still has time to care for you. Why, He even knows how many hairs you have on your head! God is faithful, and His love surrounds you. He has given you life to worship Him. At His command, your life is protected and your path secure. The dreams God has for you will never be shaken.

You are protected because of God. You thrive because of Him. You have been saved because of Him. No matter how strong a person is, without God, they have nothing. Even if they feel that a life filled with worldly treasure is enough, a day will come when everything falls apart. Without God, there is no hope. Without Him, there is no love. Without Him, there is no trust. No matter how hard a person works, without God it's all for nothing. Continue to run after Him. Find Him in every hour. See that He cares. Know that He loves you. Always.

GOD, PLEASE HELP ME NEVER TO TURN AWAY FROM THE TRUTH THAT YOU ARE FOR ME!
I WANT TO KEEP BEING BRAVE AND LIVE OUT THE DREAMS THAT YOU HAVE FOR MY LIFE.

POWER

God is the strength of my heart and all I need forever.
PSALM 73:26

The enemy tries to make you doubt God's presence in your life. He wants you to believe that God doesn't care about your needs. Satan doesn't want you to know the lengths to which God goes to pursue your soul. He doesn't want you to know that God thinks about everything you do. God keeps His eyes on you all day long. You are blessed because God has chosen you.

God has made an eternal inheritance for you, and He wants you to know just how special you are. Be brave, for He watches over you and watches out for you. He has formed your heart, and He knows every beat it takes. His desire is to love and take care of you.

Remain humble and keep relying on God. The enemy lies and says that God is not as powerful as you think. He manipulates people into thinking that God is nothing more than an idea. The enemy has sold people the notion that God is optional. Be brave and ignore the lies. Be brave and know that God is with you.

GOD, REMIND ME TO KEEP MY HOPE IN YOU. REMIND ME THAT YOUR LOVE FOR ME IS ETERNAL. THANK YOU FOR CARING ABOUT ME ALL DAY LONG.

STAND BY ME

O Lord, stand by me.
PSALM 26:1

Seek God whether the sun shines or storms rain down. No matter what you feel, God always delivers you from the enemy's lies. God will always answer you. He created you and gave you time to be with Him, both now and for all eternity. He made you to shine brightly in the dark world because you are brave and keep your eyes on Him.

You are wonderful. When God sees you, He sees His flawless design. Every time you need Him, He is there for you. There isn't a trouble that He can't save you from, so follow Him today with renewed faith in all His promises. Be brave, for His angels guard your path. They surround you. Go without fear, for you are loved.

Find God in everything you do. He is good. Find all the comfort and rest you need in Him. He is here for you. Taste the joy that comes from running after a life covered in His grace.

LORD, I WANT TO TAKE MY TROUBLES AND SET ALL OF THEM DOWN BEFORE YOU. THANK YOU FOR ALWAYS STANDING BY ME. I CAN FEEL YOU HELPING ME GET STRONG WHEN I SEEK YOU. WITH YOU, I LACK NOTHING.

PEACE THROUGH HIS STRENGTH

Give all your cares to the Lord and He will give you strength.
PSALM 55:22

God doesn't want you to live in fear; you are safe in Him. He made you to live a life that brings Him glory and you peace. He created you to love life, not just to get through each day. The enemy tells you that you're hopeless and that your dreams will never come true because God is not big enough to make them happen. Each day that God gives you comes from His good heart.

Don't entertain the enemy's lies. Run after God's goodness. Be intentional about seeking peace. In every situation, pursue it.

God is watching over you. He is always looking ahead and behind to make sure your walk with Him is protected. Jesus has made you righteous, and you are eternally important. Be brave and know that God listens to you. He hears everything you say, and it all matters to Him. His face shines on you and covers your life. The light of His glory is always on you to guide your steps. God doesn't ignore you or walk away from you.

FATHER, THANK YOU FOR NEVER LEAVING ME TO FACE MY BATTLES
ON MY OWN. THANK YOU FOR DELIVERING ME FROM EVERY ONE OF
MY TROUBLES SO THAT I MAY HAVE EVERLASTING PEACE.

24-7 GRACE

The loving-kindness of God lasts all day long.
PSALM 52:1

Take this new day and hold on to God's promises. Think of God and His great love for you. Spend today bringing Him glory. Think of ways to be a blessing to others. Introduce Jesus to someone who doesn't know Him. That could be a friend at school or church. Jesus made relationships with the people He sought to help.

The enemy wants you to see God's grace as limited, something that can help in the morning and maybe in the evening, but never all day long. He wants you to see God's mercy in the same way, like bookends far apart, holding up different parts of your day. The truth is that God's grace has given you all of this day as a gift.

A broken heart isn't a sign of weakness. It is proof of God's presence. When your spirit feels crushed under the weight of daily demands, don't forget that He is there to save you. He pulls you up from the darkness and always holds you close.

GOD, SOME DAYS IT'S HARD TO BE BRAVE. THANK YOU FOR BEING WITH ME THROUGH EVERY ONE OF THEM. THANK YOU FOR HELPING ME STAY STRONG EVEN WHEN I FEEL WEAK.

OUR STRONG PLACE

The Lord of All is with us. The God of Jacob is our strong place.
PSALM 46:11

There is no one like God. Because God created you, nothing in the world can satisfy you like He can. He is the one training you up in the ways of bravery. He is the one who rescues you when life seems too hard to handle. He is the one who defends you when the enemy is trying to steal your hope. God will not leave you alone to endure suffering.

God lifts you up and makes sure you are taken care of. He always provides for you, for He is good. Jesus saved you, so the enemy can never take you away from God. The devil's path is darkness. The pits he hopes you fall in will be filled by God's grace, so you won't be hurt by them.

Your prayers do not go unanswered. Be humble and follow God. Listen to Jesus direct your steps, and rejoice. When you stumble, God catches you before you fall. He is so pleased with you. Don't fear when it feels like the world is against you.

LORD, HELP ME TO KEEP MY HEAD UP. I WANT YOU TO BE PROUD OF THE BRAVE BOY I'M BECOMING. THANK YOU FOR ALWAYS LOVING ME.

REFLECT GOD FOR OTHERS

"The Lord will always lead you."
ISAIAH 58:11

God knows exactly what you're going through. He knows exactly what you're feeling. God has told you before and will remind you many more times that He will never leave you alone. He will never walk away and forsake you. He will never go far away and leave you wondering where He is. The Lord especially wants to strengthen you as you share the gospel with others.

God has called you to be brave and to live a life that reflects the Savior's love. Most people don't know Jesus like you do. For God's glory, be bold and tell others what He's done for you. Let your love for people be an offering that brings God praise all day long. Let your kind words to the hurting be a sacrifice of praise to God. God will continuously use you as a reflection of His love.

GOD, I DON'T WANT TO WORRY ABOUT WHAT OTHER PEOPLE THINK OF ME. I DON'T WANT TO LET THEIR OPINIONS STOP ME FROM TALKING ABOUT YOU. NO MATTER WHAT KIND OF DAY I HAVE, PLEASE HELP ME TO SPEND MY TIME REJOICING AND GIVING YOU THANKS.

FREE TO LIVE THROUGH CHRIST

Christ made us free.
GALATIANS 5:1

Don't worry about what other people think of you. Don't let their words define you, for Jesus, the Word, defines you! He is your beautiful Savior who keeps loving you no matter what the days bring. Continue to do the tasks God calls you to with a humble heart so that people will see that He is in your heart.

People worship themselves and don't even realize they're lost in a darkness that only Jesus can save them from. You matter because as you go down the path God has for you, people will hear praise and truth come from your mouth. They will see you do good things from your compassionate heart. They will see you find ways to love the unwanted. They will see Jesus in you and begin to wonder.

God's love and faithfulness reach across every part of your life. They carry you into this new day and keep you wrapped in truth. They fill you and give you confidence to stand up for God in the fallen world.

GOD, NO MATTER WHERE I GO, YOU ARE THERE FOR ME. THANK YOU FOR ALWAYS KEEPING ME CLOSE TO YOU. YOU KEEP ME GOING. GUARD MY HEART WITH YOUR LOVE THAT NEVER FAILS.

LIVE IN LOVE

*God is love. If you live in love, you live by the
help of God and God lives in you.*
1 JOHN 4:16

God's blessings for you aren't limited. He doesn't look at you and consider your mistakes before pouring out blessings. God looks at you and sees His Son. God looks at you and is pleased for the new creation Jesus has made you to be. In Him is an abundance of hope. In Him is life. Through Him your eyes have been opened to see the plans God has for you. His love for you doesn't end. It continues to fill your heart and lift you up. His presence keeps the enemy from reaching you. Follow God today and hear His voice say you are important and dearly loved!

Nothing can stand against God. You are safe under the love of His wings, which means the evil one can't get to you with his lies. Don't worry about the darkness; it can't cover you anymore. The enemy's plan to take your thoughts off God will fail. It will wither and fade away. Use the new hours that God is giving you today to wait on Him.

LORD, THANK YOU FOR THIS NEW DAY. HELP ME TO LIVE IN LOVE FOR YOU! I WANT TO
BE PATIENT, KNOWING ALL THE TIME THAT YOU ARE LEADING ME TO BE A BRAVE BOY.

MAKE GOD FAMOUS

*I will make known with my mouth how
faithful You are to all people.*
PSALM 89:1

Trust God. Trust Him to know what is best for you. Spend your time doing good for others. Whether that means listening to someone who needs to talk or sacrificing your time to help a person who needs a problem solved, do it all for God's glory. That's what being a brave young man looks like.

Your life is right in the middle of safe pastures, so you don't have to fear the enemy's schemes. Do what God says. He loves you because He is love. Find delight in Him. Let God fill your heart until love overflows and people around you see the change. Give God your life. Run after Him. Stay connected to His truth, and He will make you shine like the morning sun for His glory.

The enemy tries to steal your hope because he knows his fate is sealed. He still works to take your will and redirect it onto things of the world instead of glorifying God. The enemy hates when you make God known to others. Ask God for continued courage to spread the good news.

GOD, REMIND ME TO STAY HUMBLE AS YOU CONTINUE TO GUIDE MY PATH AND GIVE ME PEACE. HELP ME ALL DAY LONG TO LOOK FOR WAYS TO GLORIFY YOU AND YOUR WORD.

MASTER

Life began by Him. His Life was the Light for men.
JOHN 1:4

Jesus is your best example of what it means to be brave. He wasn't afraid to do the hard work it took to save your soul. He left heaven to come to earth and live as a man. Jesus loves you so much that He submitted to torture and crucifixion to become your Savior. He laid down His life for you.

Jesus loved people. That's really being brave, because some days that is hard to do. He made sure they knew they mattered. He made it a point to let others speak what was on their minds, and He listened. Don't get discouraged if you find it difficult to communicate with people. Realize that you are a child of God and that Jesus is always with you. Ask Him to help you overcome the things in life that you think are keeping you from being brave.

Jesus sacrificed His life to save yours. He allowed soldiers to spit on Him and nail Him to the cross. And after He died, Jesus conquered death by rising three days later! He is alive and cheering you on. Be brave and let Him keep being the Master of your life.

JESUS, THANK YOU FOR LOVING ME AND DOING EVERYTHING YOU DID FOR ME ON THE CROSS. PLEASE KEEP LEADING ME. IN YOUR HOLY NAME I PRAY.

STAND UP

Do not be ashamed to tell others about what our Lord said.
2 TIMOTHY 1:8

Read God's Word and consider His truth. Let His commands be enough. Let them cover you as you go about your day. Think about how He made you to do great things for His glory. Jesus is your Savior, and this new gift of today is for you to give everything to Him. Jesus is your Shepherd who guards your life, so you don't have to spend time worrying about the things you can't change. God's Word is sharper than a two-edged sword, so study your Bible and hide God's Word in your heart so that you can stand up to the enemy. Memorize God's commands and make today for lifting up the poor. Raise up the needy and let your actions remind them of their worth to God.

Don't let the enemy tempt you to set your sights on worldly treasure. He wants you to see all the big and beautiful things and begin to wish you had them for yourself. He wants you to see how cool the new and expensive video games, sports gear, and sneakers are. The devil tells you to run after these things to solve your problems. He does this because your enemy wants you to forget that Jesus has already solved your problems!

GOD, THANK YOU FOR MAKING ME A NEW CREATION. HELP ME TO BE BRAVE AND TO STAND UP FOR WHAT IS RIGHT. HELP ME TO BE MORE LIKE JESUS.

GOD CARES

Give all your worries to Him because He cares for you.
1 Peter 5:7

Spend this new day doing good for others. God is with you forever and will never forsake you. Don't let the evil one tell you that he has a better way. Jesus is the Way. Jesus made a way, and He is leading you on the path of justice. Follow Him and be blessed. Keep God's words in your heart. Let them direct your thoughts. As you go today, speak truth and know that God is protecting you from the evil one. He will always keep your feet on solid ground so you can continue doing the work He has called you to do.

God doesn't want this new day to be a burden, but an opportunity for you to fall deeper in love with His will for your life. The enemy wants you to concentrate on the world and all its false promises. He wants you to keep your eyes on temporary things that fade away. He wants you to forget that God cares for you more than anyone else. The enemy hopes that you will consider his wicked ways as a solution to your troubles. He doesn't want you to remember that Jesus has already defeated him.

LORD, HELP ME TO STAND FIRM NO MATTER WHAT HAPPENS TODAY. THANK YOU FOR CARING FOR ME.

WORTH IN CHRIST

You are living this new life for God.
ROMANS 6:11

God knows your heart. Continue to find your worth in Him and be confident that He is with you every step of the way. He makes sure that your life is always secure. The lies of the enemy can't knock you down. There might be a day when you stumble, but there will never come a day when the enemy makes you fall. Hear God remind you that His strong hands are holding you and guiding you all day long. He never takes them away, so you can be brave and not worry about anything. When the enemy tries to strike, remember that God is your strong tower. Take refuge in Him alone.

No matter what, keep your hope in Christ. Stay on the paths He is guiding you down. By the power of Jesus in you, remain upright and honest. Continue to have integrity so that others may always see a difference when they see you. Seek peace in every situation. Share the love of Jesus with everybody. Tell them all the things He has done for you. Tell them that God loves them and sent His Son to rescue them too.

GOD, REMIND ME THAT MY WORTH AND THE WORTH OF
OTHERS IS IN YOU! THANK YOU FOR LOVING ME!

BECAUSE OF JESUS

You were set apart for God-like living to do His work.
1 CORINTHIANS 6:11

Concentrate on God's love for you. Don't let each mistake pull you away from Him. Remember that when He looks at you, He sees a new creation, carefully formed from your Savior's love. When God considers your life, He doesn't shake His head at your shortcomings. He sees your heart and keeps it filled with His mercy and grace.

Because of Jesus, you have God's love with you. Because of Jesus, your sin no longer separates you from His love. Because of Jesus, God's hands hold you close. You have been made strong by the blood of the Lamb. Your soul now bears the light to shine in the darkest places. You have been made into a beautiful new creation.

Let God continue molding you into the person He made you to be. Living in a broken world means that you will have hard days. The enemy hopes you focus on these so your eyes will be turned away from God's blessings. Go about your day keeping your heart open so He can keep showing you how to be a brave boy.

THANK YOU, FATHER, FOR ALWAYS GIVING ME THE STRENGTH TO BE BRAVE AND TO HELP PEOPLE. HELP ME TO REMEMBER THAT YOU DON'T MAKE MISTAKES.

GOD'S BLESSINGS

"They will know that a man of God has been among them."
EZEKIEL 33:33

Don't let guilt keep you down. God's goal is not for you to spend your day feeling overwhelmed. He doesn't want you to trudge through each hour carrying burdens that you were never meant to carry. The heaviest burden in the world was the cross that Jesus carried to Calvary's hill. Jesus carried it for you so that on the day you believed in His holy, mighty, and perfect name, you became free from the burdens of sin. What a blessing! You were not saved to be miserable or walk around in the darkness. You were saved to be free. You were saved to be strong and to sing praises to your King with all your heart.

Don't let the enemy trick you into believing that God's voice is too quiet to be heard. Don't let him tell you that you can't hear God because of your mistakes. The devil wants nothing more than to see you become overwhelmed with grief. He wants you to have a hard time hearing God. Wait for God to answer you. He cares about every part of you. Wait for God by reading His Word and remembering all the ways He has blessed you.

GOD, THANK YOU FOR HEARING ME. I WANT TO PRAISE
YOU FOR ALL THE WAYS YOU BLESS ME.

CELEBRATE

For You have made me glad by what You have done, O Lord.
PSALM 92:4

Be brave and celebrate the life God has given you. The enemy takes pleasure in pulling you away from God. He loves to see you stumble, but God cares about keeping your feet on solid ground. God doesn't want to see you sad. Open your heart and let God take your problems. He is for you and doesn't want you to fall. The enemy wants you to concentrate on the world and look for answers in it instead of in God's Word. Hear God remind you of the truth so you will continue to run after Jesus.

Today is for enjoying God's grace, so keep walking down the path He has set you on. Feel God's love fill your heart. Don't be disappointed when things don't go your way. The enemy would like for you to live your life always feeling like you never have enough. The enemy loves to see God's children disappointed and detached from His promises. He wants you to believe that disappointments mean that God's mercy isn't long enough to reach you. But the truth is, God is holding you through every hour of every day.

THANK YOU, JESUS, FOR GIVING ME GRACE. THANK YOU FOR NEVER LEAVING ME ALONE.

HANDS HELD HIGH

I know that everything God does will last forever.
ECCLESIASTES 3:14

God treasures your life. He wants you to know how special you are. But the enemy wants you to feel defeated. He wants you to feel less than everything God has made you to be. In the times when God is calling you to be brave and to lead, the enemy wants you to feel powerless. He wants you to believe that other people don't want to follow someone like you. In the times when God calls you to love, the enemy wants you to be angry. He wants you to believe that you have a right to defend yourself with selfishness. That's not who God made you to be. The devil wants you to forget that God is your defender. He wants you to forget that God is the source of your power and strength. He wants you to forget that God's Spirit gives you the right words to say and you will be heard.

Each day is a gift, wrapped with God's mercy and grace. Keep your hope in Him and remember that He will never leave you alone. Keep your hands held high and worship Him!

GOD, I WANT TO BE BRAVE AND SET A GOOD EXAMPLE FOR
MY FRIENDS. THANK YOU FOR BLESSING MY DAYS.

DARKNESS INTO LIGHT

"I am the Light of the world. Anyone who follows Me will not walk in darkness."
John 8:12

Take each step with God. Look at His truth in the pages of your Bible. Let His commands remain in your heart. Don't forget that He hears and cares about all your prayers. Don't stop crying out to Him. On days when your spirit is full, God gives you the strength to lift your hands in praise. And when your spirit feels empty and you have nothing to give, God pours more love in. You mean everything to Him, and He will never stop reminding you of that!

Wait for God. Be brave by not letting the day's problems distract you from God's loving heart. Be patient before Him. Listen to His words and see that His face is turned to you. Don't forget how God pulled you out of the darkness and set your life on the rock. Your feet now stand firm on Jesus! What happens today doesn't matter because the enemy can't move you away from God. The Lord has given you a new song so the people around you will consider putting their trust in Jesus instead of in the empty things of the world.

GOD, THANK YOU FOR SHOWING ME WHAT TO DO. I KNOW YOU HAVE SO MANY GOOD THINGS PLANNED FOR ME. HELP ME TO BE GRATEFUL ALWAYS.

THE ONE

I did not give up waiting for the Lord.
And He turned to me and heard my cry.
PSALM 40:1

Be brave by trusting God. Nothing in the world is worth your heart. The enemy continues to tempt you into thinking that you have to work hard to get God's attention. But remember that God is the one who opened your heart to salvation. He is the one who made a way for you to inherit eternal life. He did all this in His perfect timing. Now He hears all your prayers and will answer each of them.

Make knowing God what you want more than anything. Keep His words hidden like a treasure in your heart. Let them give you the courage to boldly proclaim His love for the world. Don't live a silent life. Remind the people around you to seek God. Remind them that His love is great. God thinks of you all the time and keeps your heart from failing. His love always protects you from the enemy's schemes. He is always here to help you.

THANK YOU, GOD, FOR ALWAYS LISTENING TO ME.
PLEASE KEEP REMINDING ME OF HOW IMPORTANT I AM TO YOU!

I AM

"For I am God, and there is no other.
I am God, and there is no one like Me."
ISAIAH 46:9

Spend time looking out for people who are weak. Sacrifice your time to help someone who needs compassion. God is with you along the way and will always help. He will protect you as you serve others. As you pour out your life for the ones who need a friend, God is there to bless you. Find the people whom everyone else passes by and share the love of Jesus with them. Let them know how much they matter. God keeps your life close to His heart. Don't ever doubt His promises!

Even though you make mistakes, God still has mercy on you. Even though you stumble and fall, God is always there to help you up and heal your pain. The enemy wants you to walk around with a heavy heart. He wants you to believe that each new day is to be dreaded instead of seeing it as a chance to live in God's power and love. The devil wants you to imagine that you are alone and have to face challenges by yourself. He wants you to waste time worrying that there are some problems in life that don't have answers. But you have Jesus, God's perfect Son, who died, rose, and set you free from every sin!

LORD, YOU ARE THE GREAT I AM! THANK YOU FOR EVERYTHING YOU DO FOR ME.

LET GO

God is our safe place and our strength.
He is always our help when we are in trouble.
PSALM 46:1

Set down all your heavy burdens and put your hands in God's hands. Let everything go and rest your soul in Him. He is always with you. Be brave by making today about desiring God more than anything else. Let go of every wish and dream. Just stay with Him. He is your heavenly Father, who loves you more than anything. Let Him lead you to streams of grace where you will be able to take in blessings and never again go thirsty. Anywhere you go today, He will be there for you. Meet with Him and listen to His truth. Absorb His love and be a blessing to someone in need of compassion.

The enemy wants you to be satisfied with sadness. He wants you to forget that Jesus is your daily Bread. He wants you to forget that Jesus is your Savior. The devil tries to orchestrate events to make people think that God is absent. Be brave and resist this lie.

LORD, HELP ME TO USE THE LIGHT YOU'VE PUT IN MY HEART TO GO AND BRING YOUR MESSAGE OF HOPE TO THE ONES LIVING IN DARKNESS.

EVERLASTING GOD

For God is the King of all the earth.
PSALM 47:7

Keep your hope in God and turn to your Bible for answers. Don't walk away from Him to look for love. He did not create you to worry or fear. He made you to shine. He made you to follow His plan and lift up your hands in praise. Expect to meet with God today. Expect Him to bless you and show you just how important you are. Listen to His voice say that you are wonderful and worthy.

God is your Father who cares for you. He knows you have stressful days. Remember God and His everlasting love for you. When the noise of the world seems to wash out your quiet time with Him, know that He always hears your voice. Rely on His endless supply of grace. When the enemy's lies seem to cover up God's promise that you are forgiven, know without a doubt that God still loves you.

GOD, SOMETIMES I FEEL LIKE THE WORLD IS CRASHING OVER ME AND BEING BRAVE IS HARD. I KNOW THAT YOU ARE STRONG AND WILL HOLD BACK THE TIDES OF DOUBT FOR ME. KEEP ME SAFE IN EVERY STORM. HELP ME TO FEEL YOUR ENDLESS LOVE.

WISDOM

A wise man listens to good teaching.
PROVERBS 12:15

As you consider this new day that God has made for you, remember that He is leading and teaching you. Real wisdom and bravery come from reading your Bible and doing what it says. God directs every one of your steps with His infinite love for you. Even at night, His song of love and forgiveness is with you. Let the choices you make today be a prayer of thanksgiving to Jesus for all He has done for you. Think about the cross. Think about the day Jesus decided that you were worth it all and picked it up and carried the weight of all your sins to Golgotha. Jesus, your rock and Savior, chose to do this because of His great love for you.

God is your stronghold. Even if a day comes when you feel like God is far away, He is still your strength. He will never reject you. Don't believe the enemy's lies. God didn't give you life to walk around in sadness. He created you to be His light-bearer. God created you to be brave and to listen to Him guide you through your day.

GOD, PLEASE KEEP ME STRONG AND REMIND ME THAT YOU ARE ALWAYS BY MY SIDE. THANK YOU FOR NEVER LEAVING ME ALONE.

TALK TO GOD

You must keep praying.
COLOSSIANS 4:2

Praying is a great way to be brave and stay connected to God. He is your support, and He always defends you. Just as you spend your days telling people about Jesus and standing up for His holy name, He proclaims your name among the angels and saints. You are loved and known. When the world around you is lost in the dark, God rescues you and puts your feet on solid ground.

Keep God's words planted firmly in your heart, and let Him teach you new things today. Let Him show you how helping someone in need actually trains you to be a leader. The more you give to others, the more you actually receive.

The Holy Spirit dwells in you, so you will never be in a place without Him. Let Him continue to be everything that brings you joy. He keeps your heart beating so that you will find all of your delight in Him. Pray to Him all the time. He is your God who cares.

GOD, HELP ME TO GET BETTER AT PRAYING. HELP ME TO SEE
PRAYER AS A GREAT WAY TO STAY CONNECTED TO YOU.

YOUR KING

On His coat and on His leg is the name written,
"KING OF KINGS AND LORD OF LORDS."
REVELATION 19:16

Jesus is your King. He decides the direction of your steps. He guides you by the light of His face so you will never lose your way. He makes you thrive. Jesus holds back the enemy's armies. He gives you strength to trample Satan's wicked temptations. The enemy is powerless to put you to shame. Jesus has rescued you and set you free so you can worship God every hour of every new day. Don't put your trust in things. Keep your trust in God. Remember that you have been redeemed by Jesus paying the price for your sins. He is the only one worthy to call Messiah, so make each day count for His name's sake. Praise His glorious and holy name forever.

The enemy will try to make you believe that God has turned His back on you. He will try to make you feel powerless and alone. Reject Satan's lies and hold on to God's promises.

THANK YOU, JESUS, FOR DYING FOR ME. THANK YOU FOR CHOOSING ME TO BE A LIGHT FOR YOUR GLORY. THANK YOU FOR CAUSING ME TO SHINE.

WONDERFUL HEART

"For the Lord your God is the One Who goes with you."
DEUTERONOMY 20:4

Your life matters. Jesus shed His blood so that every one of your sins would be forgiven. Let this truth soak in, because when the love of Jesus is in you, nothing can make you feel "less than" or unwanted. The enemy wants you to feel those things so that your focus will be taken off of God. He wants you to think that people look at you and see something shameful. God does not make mistakes. What God sees when He looks at you is all that matters. In you, God sees a beautiful spirit with a lot to give. In you, God sees a wonderful heart that beats for truth and grace. Best of all, when God considers your life, He sees Jesus.

In this new day, use the love and strength God has given you to make a difference in someone's life. A simple gesture of compassion can be enough to remind a person of God's presence in his life. As you bless someone else, don't forget how much God loves you too. Keep your eyes on Jesus. He is your rock, and He will always hold your heart in His mighty hands.

JESUS, I WANT TO BECOME A LEADER. HELP ME TO LIVE AND PRAY LIKE YOU. HELP ME TO CARE ABOUT OTHERS THE WAY YOU DO.

GOD GOES BEFORE YOU

"I will trust and not be afraid. For the Lord
God is my strength and song."
ISAIAH 12:2

God has not forgotten you. While you go about working on the plans He is calling you to, He is keeping the enemy from oppressing you. God will prevent the devil's lies from taunting you, and He will always remind you that your worth is in Him.

Consider all of God's promises. Just as God used His hands to form you and give you life, He also uses them to drive out the enemy. He cares about you so much that He crushes the enemy's plans to take your attention off God. When Satan tries to lure you away from God's heart, God thwarts his efforts. It is because of God's power that you are victorious against the devil's temptations. Turn your face to God and see that He is always good. He goes before you. Remember this, because the enemy will tempt you to live for yourself. He wants you to forget that it is because of God's love that you have success.

You live in the middle of grace and forgiveness. When the enemy says that God has rejected you, remember that the truth is you have been rescued and are forever free.

LORD, I PRAY THAT YOU WOULD BLESS ME AND SHOW ME
HOW TO BE MORE LIKE JESUS EVERY DAY.

MANY BLESSINGS

The Lord will give strength to His people.
The Lord will give His people peace.
PSALM 29:11

Take time today to let God's words soak into your soul. Let His teachings stir you to a boldness that will carry you to new people. Be brave and bring them the love of Jesus with your words and actions. Tell them that God is faithful and declare His goodness to those who are hurting. God has filled your heart with grace so you will have courage to stand up for His name when others around you do not.

Your hands and feet are powerful tools. Use them for God's glory, to reach people in need. Hold their requests in your heart as you pray. Guide them to the cross and rejoice with the angels as you witness God's saving grace redeem their souls.

God has blessed you and will continue to bless you forever. From all His majesty and splendor, He brings you victory in resisting the enemy's lies.

GOD, THANK YOU FOR MAKING ME BRAVE. LIKE JESUS, I WANT TO BE HONEST AND HUMBLE. I DON'T WANT TO BE DEFENSIVE AND ANGRY. PLEASE HELP ME TO MAKE THE CHANGES I NEED TO MAKE SO I CAN LOOK MORE LIKE JESUS.

BEAUTIFUL

"Look to the Lord and ask for His strength.
Look to Him all the time."
1 CHRONICLES 16:11

When God looks at you, He sees a beautiful person. You are beautiful and forgiven because of Jesus! Don't waste this new day trying to be someone else. Forget what others say is beautiful. You have been made into a new creation, and now Jesus radiates from your heart. People look at you and see what God's Son has done.

Pay attention to God's promises and listen to Him for direction. Don't worry about what other people say. Your worth and identity are in God alone. Continue to honor Him with your righteous living. Honor Him with your words of kindness and generous deeds. Hear God remind you that you mean everything to Him. Don't depend on the promises of others, and don't expect people to fill your desire for approval. Run to Jesus. In Him you will be perfectly satisfied.

Keep reading your Bible so that God's Word will continue to encourage you and give you understanding. Remain humble, and show others a difference. Keep following God and be the one who stands up for justice.

LORD, I PRAY THAT MY LIFE WILL SHOW OTHERS WHO YOU REALLY ARE.
KEEP GUIDING ME AND SHOWING ME THE RIGHT WAYS TO GO.

DO IT FOR JESUS

"For God can do all things."
LUKE 1:37

God tramples the enemy's armies so that you are able to achieve the plans God has designed for you. His kingdom will last forever. He has adopted you, and together you will be Father and child forever!

Let everything you do today be done for Jesus. He is your King. Honor Him with your work. Use the love He has given you to reach out and change the world for His glory. You are brave, and many look to you for guidance because they know your help comes from God. Jesus has made you glorious, a precious light in this very dark world. Honor Him with your love for others, even the ones who seem to be against you.

Your life is to make God's name known across the land. Make your mark for Him on your generation, following the same path God's children have done throughout every generation. Focus on making Jesus known today. Let the work of your hands reflect the goodness of His loving heart so that the nations will bring Him glory for all time.

GOD, THANK YOU FOR SAVING ME. YOUR GRACE IS A PRICELESS
GIFT. HELP ME TO SHARE IT WITH THOSE IN NEED OF JESUS.

BRAVE WITH THE LORD

The name of the Lord is a strong tower.
The man who does what is right runs into it and is safe.
PROVERBS 18:10

God loves you, and He is your safe place. Come to Him in good and bad times, for He is always with you. His presence in your life means that you don't have to worry about solving problems on your own. Yes, you will have problems, but the Holy Spirit is with you to keep you from falling. The power you need today comes from Him. Even on the days when it feels like everything is falling apart and you're not sure what to do, He is there to protect you. The enemy will try to whisper that bad things happen because God has walked away from you. Stay with God and let Him take care of you.

The enemy doesn't stop. If he can't distract you with lies, he will try to get you to focus on your struggles. He won't remind you that they're temporary. He won't remind you that God is more powerful than all of your struggles combined and that you are powerful too because His Holy Spirit is in you. Even on the days when it feels like the mountains of your faith quake, you'll be okay because God loves you.

THANK YOU, JESUS, FOR TELLING ME EVERYTHING IS GOING
TO BE OKAY. HELP ME TO KEEP BEING BRAVE!

THE WAY

"I have kept His way and have not turned aside."
JOB 23:11

Brave people hunger for God and know without a doubt that He is with them forever. Know that God is mighty. He is strong enough to handle any problem you will face. He is your fortress. In Him you are safe from the enemy's advances. God rises up around you to keep your life guarded from insecurity and shame. Open His Word and see all the times He has given His children strength to overcome adversity. Your life is completely secure in God. Stand tall today on these truths and believe that He is holding your life in His hands.

Desire God's plans for your life instead of forging your own path. Trust Him. Spend your day sharing all the things He has done for you. Be bold and tell others how God has been faithful in keeping His promises. As you go about the work He has for you, be encouraged, knowing that God is your defender. He is not sending you out into the world alone.

GOD, HELP ME TO HEAR YOUR VOICE REMIND ME THAT I AM STRONG ENOUGH WITH YOU. THANK YOU FOR HELPING ME STAY TRUE TO YOUR WAY. I KNOW THAT THE ENEMY NO LONGER HAS INFLUENCE OVER ME.

POWERFUL

David became greater and greater,
for the Lord God of All was with him.
2 SAMUEL 5:10

Today is here for God to help you. These new hours are for Him to keep you from falling. He will remind you that even though the world's kingdoms fall, He is always lifting you up. Concentrate on God's character. Remember that He is faithful and just and trustworthy. Listen to His voice and hear the new song of mercy He has for you. Let His words melt away your stress and fear.

Be still before God. Study your Bible and learn more about His character. Know that He cares about you more than anyone. Let your life exalt His holy name. Be intentional about remembering all the things He has done for you. He is answering your prayers. See that He has been faithful in keeping His promises. See that He is powerful enough to stop your doubting. He stops the enemy who tries to wage war against you. He breaks the bow of sadness and shatters the spears of regret.

FATHER, THANK YOU FOR LETTING ME KNOW HOW STRONG I AM
BECAUSE OF JESUS. PLEASE LEAD ME IN THE WAY YOU WANT ME
TO GO. I'M SORRY WHEN I MESS UP. PLEASE FORGIVE ME.

READY TO SAVE

Who is this One Who is beautiful in His clothing, walking in the greatness of His strength? "It is I, Who speaks what is right and good, powerful to save."
ISAIAH 63:1

Let everything you do bring God glory. Let everything you do bring Him praise. Join in the chorus of saints who live to make God famous. From this moment until the day's end, concentrate on worship. People who see you worship God will begin to think about life. They will hear your words of praise and see your hands help the needy. They will wonder about God, and you will tell them. Be brave and go out into your world and be a blessing to someone who is trying to find truth. Tell them that Jesus is ready to save.

God is on His throne. He is King over all the earth. You have nothing to fear because His love keeps you secure. Let your choices honor Him, for He is worthy of all your praise. Turn these new hours into worship, and let your voice be heard among the nations. Don't feel like you aren't good enough or worthy enough to do great things for God and His kingdom!

GOD, I WANT TO HEAR JESUS SPEAK LOVE AND POWER INTO MY HEART. THANK YOU FOR ALWAYS REMINDING ME THAT I AM VERY IMPORTANT AND DEARLY LOVED BY YOU. HELP ME TO BE YOUR WITNESS IN THE WORLD.

STAND WITH JESUS

"Stand up and give honor and thanks to the
Lord your God forever and ever!"
NEHEMIAH 9:5

The enemy is trying to get you to focus on worldly treasures. He wants you to feel incomplete. He wants you to spend your time collecting and hoarding things. But don't forget, God is your fortress. In Him you have everything you will ever need. He is in you and He is above all things. He is worthy of your heart because He sent Jesus to die for it. He paid the price so that your sins could be washed away.

God wants you to focus on His beautiful creation. See His radiance shine from the sun. Feel His approval from a friend's kind word. Look at mountains and consider that His power made them rise. Spread the joy you get from God throughout your whole day.

The enemy wants you to feel like you stand alone. He wants you to believe that you only have yourself to rely on. The enemy tries to make you think that your bad days will never end. He hopes that you will live in a place where you always feel overwhelmed and outnumbered. But you stand with Jesus!

JESUS, HELP ME TO RELY ON YOU. I WANT TO BE BRAVE.
I WANT TO BE A LEADER. THANK YOU FOR ALWAYS HELPING ME.

CLOSER TO JESUS

He will feed His flock like a shepherd. He will gather the lambs in His arms and carry them close to His heart.
ISAIAH 40:11

See today as a new opportunity to be closer to God. He wants you to understand that His love and care for you go far beyond anything you can comprehend. He is here with you. Everything is going to be okay. Your life is now forever secure in God's hands, and nothing will ever take you away from Him. The enemy wants you to believe that God only cares for you if you work hard and avoid making mistakes. Satan wants you to grab hold of his lies that make you feel abandoned and afraid. God will call you to step out of your comfortable routine some days, but He will always go before you to make your path straight. He has planned all your days, so you can know that He cares about you.

Because of Jesus, you are secure and free. You no longer have to worry about doing more to feel accepted. You don't have to wonder if God's love for you is forever. You have been set free to sing a new song of thanksgiving. So let your praises ring.

LORD, I NEED YOU. THANK YOU FOR MAKING ALL OF MY DAYS SECURE.
I WANT TO USE EVERY ONE OF THEM FOR YOUR GLORY.

MAKE TIME

"I will bring him near, and he will come close to Me."
JEREMIAH 30:21

God doesn't want you to be nervous. Don't focus on the unknowns. Concentrate on the fact that with Jesus, you are courageous. See that God has always been with you and always will be. Even when you make mistakes, God won't walk away—He never will. When you sin and the devil is there to declare you a failure, God is there to shatter his lies. When you make a choice that you know was wrong, God doesn't love you less. The enemy wants you to feel shame, but God's grace reminds you that He forgives.

Make time to read the stories and lessons God has given you. That way you will know that He doesn't withhold anything on the days you feel weighed down with guilt and frustration. He is with you today and will be with you tomorrow. Don't believe the enemy's lie that you are not worthy of all the awesome plans God has for you. Find peace in the life God has given you. He has made you to accomplish specific tasks in a special way that no one else can. You are that special to Him!

THANK YOU, GOD, FOR HELPING ME SPEND MORE AND MORE TIME WITH YOU. TEACH ME HOW TO BE BRAVER TODAY THAN I WAS YESTERDAY.

EVERY STEP

"You are to go to all the world and preach the Good News to every person."
MARK 16:15

Take time throughout this new day to hear God's voice. Read His words and listen as He teaches you more about the ways you can be brave. Listen as He tells you more about His limitless mercy and grace. The more truth about His character you absorb, the less you will worry about the things you can't control. As you continue to read your Bible and learn more about how great His love is for you, find strength in all His promises. Trusting God is the act that reminds your heart that He is your ultimate treasure. Know that believing Him will remind your soul that Jesus is more than all the world's greatest riches.

Let every step you take bring you closer to telling your friends that Jesus is their beautiful Redeemer. Tell your friends that they can't save themselves. Remind them that no one but Jesus can be their Savior. Nothing they can do is enough. Jesus is the one who paid the ultimate price for their salvation. Tell them that He is their only answer.

GOD, GIVE ME COURAGE AND STRENGTH TO TELL MY FRIENDS THAT JESUS IS GREATER THAN ANY TREASURE THEY CAN FIND IN THE WORLD. I'M SO THANKFUL THAT JESUS IS MY SAVIOR!

RISE UP

Rise up and help us! Save us because of Your loving-kindness.
PSALM 44:26

Jesus is on His throne and is King over all the earth. You have nothing to fear because His love keeps you secure. Let your choices honor Him, for He is worthy of all your praise. Turn these new hours into worship, and praise the Lord out loud. Don't feel like you aren't good enough or worthy enough to do great things for God and His kingdom. Hear Jesus speak love and power into your heart. You are very important, and you are dearly loved.

Continue to be humble and serve others, regardless of who they are. Continue to be a light for Jesus. Go to everyone with the gospel; bring light to their darkness. The enemy wants you to look at people and think they will not listen to you, but God wants you to look at them and remember Jesus. Let your heart beat by His truth so that people will know you are a child of God.

Listen to God instruct you in the way you should go. Then you won't fail when the enemy tries to pull you away to focus on your own dreams.

GOD, LET ME SHOW OTHERS HOW MUCH YOU LOVE THEM BY SHARING THE GOOD NEWS ABOUT THE DEATH AND RESURRECTION OF JESUS!

WONDER

"Give thanks to the Lord of All, for the Lord is good. His loving-kindness lasts forever."
JEREMIAH 33:11

Let everything you do bring God glory. Let everything you do bring Him praise. Join in the chorus of saints who live their lives to make God famous. From this moment until the day's end, concentrate on worship. People who hear you talk about God will begin to think about their lives. They will hear your words and think about God. They will wonder about Him, and you will have a chance to share the gospel. Go out into your world and be a blessing to someone who is trying to find truth. Tell that person Jesus is still ready to save.

God's love for you endures forever. Because of Jesus, you will do the same. He is your Shepherd, and He leads you in all the ways of His righteousness. The enemy wants you to focus on accumulating things because he wants you to rely on worldly riches instead of the riches of God's heart. He wants you to get distracted doing all kinds of things and to rely on your own strength instead of on God. Jesus is worth more than anything because He gave everything for you. Think about Him all day long. Trust in Him because He alone is worthy.

LORD, PLEASE HELP ME TO BE BRAVE. HELP ME TO TELL
PEOPLE ABOUT HOW AWESOME JESUS IS.

NEW PASTURES

I cry to You, O Lord.
JOEL 1:19

Because Jesus redeemed your life from the pit, God is giving you this new day to live unchained from yesterday's mistakes. He is drawing you closer across every hour of every day. Your sin doesn't build a river between you and God. When you make a mistake and ask for forgiveness, the love of Jesus flows like a river from His heart to yours.

Follow Jesus, your righteous Shepherd. Let Him forgive you and take away your shame. Let Jesus show you how He takes your regrets and shapes them into a beautiful future of hope.

God has blessed you by giving you the Holy Spirit, who gives you understanding. Let His words soak into your soul. Let His promises be your source of strength. They will remain your shelter in a world of uncertainty. Let Him lift you out of despair and carry you to new pastures of peace and security. Follow Him and you will not be overwhelmed. You are forgiven, and today you will enjoy the light of life because you are God's dearly loved child!

LORD, THANK YOU FOR CARING ABOUT ME. THANK YOU FOR HELPING ME GET THROUGH ALL OF LIFE'S PROBLEMS. I AM SO GLAD YOU SENT JESUS TO SAVE ME!

GROW IN CHRIST

Grow in the loving-favor that Christ gives you. Learn to know our Lord Jesus Christ better. He is the One Who saves.
2 PETER 3:18

God loves you. From the very first rays of morning sun to the last drops of light, His grace shines over you. Christ longs for you to grow strong and mature in His loving-favor.

His perfect beauty is reflected in creation. His passion for you and your well-being is like a fire that goes before you and consumes the enemy's temptations. God protects you. God considers how important you are and thinks about you all day long. Let these truths fill your heart with gladness. He is coming to you today with great things because you are His, and He wants you to know that He will never abandon you. Don't let the enemy tell you that God doesn't care. God loves every part of you and cares about everything that you hold close to your heart.

God loves justice. He fights for you. Be still and listen to His instructions. Read His Word and feel His love for you hold you close. Let this new day be a fresh start. Let it be your new sacrifice of dreams and pride so that you are free to receive all the blessings and plans He has for you.

LORD, HELP ME TO BE STILL LONG ENOUGH TO HEAR FROM YOU.
HELP ME TO BE BRAVE SO I CAN DO GREAT THINGS FOR YOU!

FINISHED

"May the one the Lord loves live by Him and be safe. The Lord covers him all the day long."
DEUTERONOMY 33:12

Jesus finished all the work required to save your soul. He paid the highest price for your heart. All you need to do to have your sins forgiven is turn away from them. The Bible calls this "repentance." When you turn your back on your sins and go the other way, Jesus washes you clean and makes you new.

Remember that God doesn't need anything that you have to offer, but He wants you and your wonderful heart. No matter how you feel, you are God's beloved child.

Don't believe the enemy's lie that God is not big enough to handle all your problems. Don't believe the lie that God is not strong enough to carry you through your current struggles. Let God complete the good works He has started in you. Everything is going to be okay. Remember that your relationship with God is a covenant of love and forgiveness.

Don't stay quiet because you feel bad about messing up. That's why Jesus went to the cross for you. God promises that He will always deliver you. In return, use your forgiven life to honor Him. Let people know that God is waiting to forgive them too.

GOD, LET ME HOLD YOUR HAND AS YOU GUIDE ME THROUGH THIS DAY.

GOD SEES

The Lord looks from heaven. He sees all the sons of men.
PSALM 33:13

Spend time praising God for all the blessings He has given you. The Lord is always able to see us, and He loves watching us give praise to Him.

Cherish His instructions more than anything. Keep listening to His voice and let His words guide you. When you see the enemy sneaking on the path, resist his temptations. Don't give in to his lies about your real worth in Jesus. Stay in community with other believers, and use your words to give God praise. Let people hear your salvation song of thanks. Go and help your brothers and sisters in need. They will see God when they see you because your life will be a beautiful reflection of God's mercy and grace.

The enemy wants you to forget about God in times of trouble. He doesn't want you to remember that God's watchful eye is always looking out for you. He surely doesn't want you apologizing to God, because the enemy is all about prideful living. The Lord has shown you salvation by sending Jesus to die for all your sins. The enemy wants you to forget this. He wants you to stay rooted in your shame and not call on Jesus. Believe God when He says you are forgiven.

LORD, PLEASE HEAR MY PRAYER. THANK YOU FOR WATCHING OVER ME. I LOVE YOU.

GOD KNOWS

"You are a God Who sees."
GENESIS 16:13

A woman named Hagar was going to have a baby. Things did not go well for her while she was pregnant. She had a lot of stress in her life, and she was sad. One day Hagar was by a well in the desert. The Bible says that the angel of the Lord found Hagar and comforted her with reassuring words. Hagar was brave and trusted that God really cared about her. She said to God, "You are a God Who sees."

From the time God created you, He has desired your heart. He doesn't make mistakes. He longs for you to grow in wisdom. The enemy wants you to believe that God can't see your heart through your sins. He wants you to feel trapped in sadness. He wants you to waste time worrying that God won't forgive you. But just as with Hagar, God sees what you're going through. Be brave and know that He doesn't hold grudges. He does hold judgment, but He has already declared you forgiven. By the blood of the Lamb you have been made new!

LORD, EVEN THOUGH I WILL STILL MAKE MISTAKES, THANK YOU FOR UNDERSTANDING AND FORGIVING ME. HELP ME TO REPENT AND FOLLOW YOU. I BELIEVE THAT YOUR FORGIVENESS CLEANSES MY HEART. THANK YOU FOR WATCHING OVER ME!

WITH GOD'S HELP

"O Lord, hear the prayer of Your servant and the prayer of Your servants who are happy to fear Your name."
NEHEMIAH 1:11

A man named Nehemiah was very brave. He was strongly connected to God and did a great thing to bring God glory. The city of Jerusalem had been attacked, and the beautiful wall around it had been destroyed. Nehemiah wanted to rebuild the wall so God's people could be protected. But to do that, Nehemiah had to be brave and ask a foreign king for help. All along the way, Nehemiah prayed. He was successful in rebuilding the wall because he put God's will first!

God is always here to help you too! He is always with you to show you the way. What can you do that will help God's people? What project can you do that will show people how awesome God is? Ask God for direction and believe that He will help you!

Your chains are gone, but the devil wants you to keep putting them back on. See this new day as an opportunity to walk closer to God and to let Him show you brand-new ways of looking at the world. Let Him guide you as He trains you up to be a brave young boy.

LORD, THANK YOU FOR THE STORY OF NEHEMIAH. I WANT TO BE MORE LIKE HIM IN THE WAY HE WAS BRAVE AND BOLD.

YOUR SHIELD

The Lord is my strength and my safe cover.
My heart trusts in Him, and I am helped.
PSALM 28:7

God has given you new life to rejoice and be brave with a glad heart. Draw close to Him and remember all the promises He has made to you. He will renew your tired spirit and make it strong again. He promises to forgive you and take away your sins because He always keeps His word. You are a treasure to Him, and He loves you.

God's presence is with you and will be with you forever. He will never cast you away or forget about you. His Holy Spirit is with you, and that will never change. Today He wants you to experience more of Him. He has proved Himself faithful, so no matter what you're feeling, know that He is here to give you more of His unfailing love. In these new hours that He has gifted you with, find more hope and know that He is here to bring you joy. This is the same joy that you experienced on the day of your salvation. Today He will give you a brave spirit so you can be strong and resist the enemy's lies.

THANK YOU, FATHER, FOR GIVING ME GRACE TO BE YOUR VOICE IN A DARK AND BROKEN WORLD. HELP ME SHOW PEOPLE HOW TO GET TO THE CROSS OF JESUS!

MESSIAH

A voice came from heaven and said, "You are My much-loved Son. I am very happy with You."
MARK 1:11

Be courageous and tell people that Jesus is the Savior. Be in the habit of speaking His sweet name, and tell those who will listen that God is here to break their chains of guilt. Tell the story of His love for their hearts. Sing songs of God's unfailing love for the brokenhearted. In the middle of trials, praise Jesus' name so that people will know He is big enough to solve their problems too.

The enemy wants to wear you down with lies that you have to work long and hard to earn God's approval. He wants you to get lost sacrificing your time for God. He wants you to get wrapped up in doing things, but what God wants from you is a heart that seeks forgiveness.

God will always go before you, so do not fear. He is protecting you from the enemy's traps. He will prosper you and build you up. The enemy can't reach you here in the shadow of God's wings.

DEAR JESUS, THANK YOU FOR BEING MY MESSIAH. THANK YOU FOR SAYING I'M SPECIAL! HELP ME TO BE BRAVE AND CONFIDENT THAT I AM YOUR WONDERFUL CREATION.

GREAT LOVE

The Lord came to us from far away, saying,
"I have loved you with a love that lasts forever."
JEREMIAH 31:3

Being brave means living a humble life. Only boast of the mighty name of Jesus and all that He has done for you. Boast of His great love all day long. The enemy tells the world that Jesus was just a good man. The enemy deceives people so they will remain blind to God's great love. He wants them to roam around in the dark and miss the gift God has for them. The enemy wants people to be content with material things. Bring hope to broken souls. Don't let harmful words get in the way of you sharing your story. When the devil says you're not worthy enough to be God's light in the darkness, hear God tell you that you are worthy because Jesus saved your soul and made you a new creation.

Take the gift of today and build people up. Help them find their ultimate worth in the cross of Jesus. Be bold and tell them about grace. Lead them to Jesus. Use your words to bring hope to the hopeless. Use your life to bring grace to the sinner. Let mercy be your guide.

JESUS, I PRAY THAT PEOPLE WILL SEE PROOF OF THE CROSS WHEN THEY LOOK AT MY LIFE!

SAVIOR

But as for me, I will watch for the Lord. I will wait for the God Who saves me. My God will hear me.
MICAH 7:7

God is the one who made a way for your salvation. He made you, and Jesus died to save you. By His grace and the blood of Jesus, your sins have been washed away. By God's power, you have been justified.

While you're worshipping God on Sunday, the enemy leaves you alone because He knows your heart feels full of joy. So He waits until you start wondering about God. He waits until you sin and then attacks you with lies. He tries to convince you that God doesn't hear your prayers so that you will feel hopeless. He tries to deceive you into thinking that because you still sin, God is ashamed of you.

Don't listen to any of this, because what Jesus did on the cross for you is truth! He loved you so much that He chose a criminal's death even though He didn't deserve it. Jesus did this so you could be set free from the chains of sin. It's because of Him that you are truly alive. Because of Jesus, God hears every one of your prayers and forgives every one of your sins. Because of His great love for you, you stand before God today unashamed and brand-new!

THANK YOU, GOD, FOR ALWAYS HELPING ME.
THANK YOU FOR ALWAYS KEEPING ME SAFE.

FOREVER

You cried to me in trouble, and I saved you.
PSALM 81:7 NLT

God knows that you are surrounded by people who don't care about Him. Don't let their behavior discourage you from bravely running after Him. Keep your heart in His truth. Don't spend your freedom worrying. Instead, praise God, for He is good. Praise Him because He has delivered you from all your troubles. Don't spend your freedom chaining yourself back to sin. Grace covers you now. Remember that God loves you and you are His forever!

God hears your prayers. Every one of them. He really cares about what you're going through. Tell Him everything and believe that He is there for you. The enemy wants you to think that God ignores you. He wants you to feel that your pleas for answers to prayer don't matter. He doesn't want you to remember that you are God's special creation and that your heart is important to God. God doesn't like it when you are sad, but the truth of what Jesus did for you is not a feeling. It's a fact. God is love for you when you're sad. He is hope for you when you're having a bad day. He is grace for you when you fail.

GOD, THANK YOU FOR LISTENING TO ME. THANK YOU FOR
MAKING ME. HELP ME TO DO THE RIGHT THING.

GOD'S CHILD

He welcomed all who visited him, boldly proclaiming the Kingdom of God and teaching about the Lord Jesus Christ.
ACTS 28:30–31 NLT

Even though you've been doing a great job of being brave, God knows that you will have doubts. The enemy is the source of all of them. He wants you to go about your day wondering if God really is there for you. He tries to threaten your faith, but you know the truth. You know that you are loved and cared for. You know that God calls you His child. Don't let the enemy's accusations erase the love God has given you. You know that your heart is safe in His hands. Don't let the enemy speak sadness into your life, because Jesus has set you free and given you His joy. That truth is where your strength comes from. Jesus is the reason you can rejoice today.

God loves you and has planned out what is best for you. Rest in the blessings that He gives you. Be satisfied with Him and the plans He has for your life.

GOD, THERE ARE TIMES WHEN I FEEL CONFUSED. THERE ARE MOMENTS WHEN I FEEL LIKE YOUR FORGIVENESS ISN'T STRONG ENOUGH TO REACH MY HEART. THE ENEMY TRIES TO CONVINCE ME TO SOLVE MY OWN PROBLEMS. THANK YOU FOR PROMISING ALWAYS TO LOVE ME!

GOD IS HERE

"Don't be afraid!"
MATTHEW 28:10 NLT

God didn't make you to run away, and He didn't create you to hide your feelings. Don't forget how special you are to Him. Doubt is the devil's playground. Guilt is his weapon of choice. He wants you to focus on the storm, but God is here for you to hold on to. In God you will find rest and forgiveness. In Him alone, you will find mercy and grace. And while you do, know that He is protecting your heart from the troubles the enemy puts in your way.

The wicked one tries to confuse you by twisting God's words. He wants struggles and strife to be people's focus. He prowls around your heart, whispering lies about your identity. You can hear him say that you are a mistake and that no matter how much good you do, things won't change. The enemy wants you to fail and feel bad about your failures. He wants to destroy your hope and faith in God. Don't let him get a foothold in your life. Remain in God. In the middle of hard things, cling to God and His words. He will never let go of you or let you down.

THANK YOU, JESUS, FOR TEACHING ME HOW TO BE A BRAVE BOY.
THANK YOU FOR REMINDING ME THAT YOU ARE NOT THE SOURCE OF
DOUBTS. YOU ARE MY SOURCE OF COURAGE AND CONFIDENCE!

SAVED FOR THE KINGDOM

"My kingdom is not of this world."
JOHN 18:36 NIV

God knows there are times when your heart feels overwhelmed with the problems you face. Remember, He is with you. He hears your cries for help. He is your God and you are His treasure, so He will get you through every struggle. The enemy wants you to focus on the battle because even he knows that your Savior, Jesus, has already won the war!

Keep your heart tuned to God's promises. You are not a burden to God. You are His, and you are forgiven. Your weariness doesn't mean that He has abandoned you. He knows how hard the hours can get, but don't forget that Jesus is here to give you peace.

Your feelings change, but God does not. The enemy wants you to misunderstand this truth. He wants you to think that because you are upset about your mistakes that God is upset with you. Your enemy wants you to stay upset at yourself so that you won't spend time realizing just how much God loves you. For your special heart, God sent Jesus into the world. For your unique soul, God gave Jesus to be your Savior. God made you for His glory, and He doesn't make mistakes.

THANK YOU, JESUS, FOR SAVING ME SO THAT I CAN LIVE IN YOUR HEAVENLY KINGDOM. PLEASE KEEP MAKING ME BRAVE. HELP ME TO TELL PEOPLE HOW AWESOME YOU ARE.

HIS LOVE

Let those who fear the Lord say,
"His loving-kindness lasts forever."
PSALM 118:4

Being brave means that instead of dwelling on what you didn't do right, you dwell in the arms of Jesus. Stay with Him and let your heart beat praise, not fear. God's glory covers the earth, even the exact place you're in right now. God doesn't walk away. He is not like men, whose hearts are full of selfishness and pride. He is not like men, who make mistakes and hurt you. God promises never to bring you harm. Remain in His words that say He has made you wonderful and that Jesus has saved you completely. You have nothing more to seek. Jesus gave everything for you, so right now you can know how much you are loved and needed.

God defends you. He is the one who guards your life and walks through every disaster with you. Stay close to God by prayer and know that He is sending you His love. Please don't let the enemy trick you. He is a skilled debater and is good at making you feel that your sins erase God's favor. He wants guilt to be your downfall. When you are tired and weak and sorrowful, God's love saves you every time.

LORD, THANK YOU FOR BEING WITH ME. HELP ME TO MAKE
PRAYING AND READING MY BIBLE A PRIORITY!

THE LIGHT

*He came to tell what he knew about the Light so
that all men might believe through him.*
JOHN 1:7

A very brave man named John the Baptist told anyone who would listen about Jesus. He lived a very simple life by the Jordan River and spent all his days telling people that Jesus was their Messiah. He baptized the people who believed. Many made fun of John and challenged him, but he never quit doing what he knew God had called him to do.

Because he spoke with such authority, the crowds kept asking John if he was the Messiah, but he said his job was to prepare the way for Jesus. One day something very special happened. Jesus was in line to be baptized by John! Can you imagine what John felt? John said, "See! The Lamb of God Who takes away the sins of the world!" (John 1:29).

As you keep working on being a brave young boy, remember John the Baptist and how he didn't let people's unkind words distract him from doing the job God had called him to do. God is on your side!

LORD, HELP ME TO BE BOLD AND BRAVE LIKE JOHN. HELP ME NOT TO GET SHY OR WORRY ABOUT MESSING UP. I WANT TO BE THE LIGHT SHINING FOR YOU IN THIS BROKEN WORLD.

LEARN FROM JESUS

He who puts his trust in the Son has life that lasts forever.
JOHN 3:36

Think about all the things God has been teaching you. You have been working hard learning how to be a brave young boy. You know that trusting Jesus is one of your biggest tools in remaining brave.

Jesus had a group of twelve friends who were called His disciples. That word means "learner." One of the men was a tax collector, and some of the others were fishermen. They were all very brave and put Jesus ahead of their jobs and families. They trusted that living for Jesus was the very best life possible.

The disciples learned daily from Jesus, and with your Bible open you can do the same thing! They saw how Jesus always treated people with love and respect. They saw Him give up His life to save theirs. They spent three years being with Jesus and watching Him do whatever it took to bring God glory. Jesus wants you to do the same thing today. Learn from Him and keep being brave!

LORD, THANK YOU FOR TEACHING ME HOW TO BE BRAVE. HELP ME STAY COMMITTED TO READING MY BIBLE AND LEARNING MORE ABOUT HOW JESUS TREATED PEOPLE SO I CAN DO THE SAME. PLEASE KEEP GUIDING MY STEPS SO I CAN BE MORE AND MORE LIKE JESUS.

DO THE RIGHT THING

Do as God would do.
EPHESIANS 5:1

Being brave means being grateful for everything God has done for you. Once when Jesus was going to Jerusalem, ten men who had leprosy, a contagious skin disease, called out to Him and asked Him to take pity on them. Jesus didn't immediately heal them but instead told them to go show themselves to the local religious leaders. The men must have been confused but obeyed Jesus anyway.

On their way, the men were miraculously healed. Only one of the men turned back to thank Jesus. The Bible says he praised God in a loud voice. After that, the man fell on his face at the feet of Jesus and thanked Him too. Jesus told the man to get up and go on his way. He said, "Your trust in God has healed you" (Luke 17:19).

Being thankful for all the things God has given you will keep you in a humble position. It will also help you stay brave. Keep your trust in Him.

LORD, I AM THANKFUL FOR EVERY BLESSING YOU HAVE GIVEN ME. HELP ME TO STAY THAT WAY. I WANT ALWAYS TO BE LIKE THE MAN WHO RETURNED TO JESUS AND EXPRESSED HIS GRATITUDE. THANK YOU, JESUS!

CARPENTER AND SAVIOR

Love means that we should live by obeying His
Word. From the beginning He has said in His
Word that our hearts should be full of love.
2 JOHN 1:6

Jesus grew up learning how to be a carpenter. He had a normal, routine handyman skill set even though He was the Savior of the world! From the beginning, Jesus was modeling the importance of hard work.

Right now, while you're still in school, your job is to work hard. See your report card as your paycheck. Being brave means caring about everything you do. The Bible even says to do everything as if you're doing it for Jesus. God understands that some days won't seem to make sense. But He is always there to help you through the hard times so your light can shine even brighter in the dark world.

Even though Jesus was a carpenter, He was still the Savior of the world! Even though you are young, God still can do amazing things through you. The secret is to love. Jesus had love in His heart, and He obeyed God's rules. Jesus loved others as He did His Father's work. You can do the same thing. Be brave and shine!

LORD, HELP ME TO STAY EXCITED TO BE BRAVE. EVEN WHEN I'M IN THE MIDDLE OF A BORING DAY, HELP ME TO SEE EACH DAY AS A GIFT. HELP ME TO BE MORE LIKE JESUS.

KEEP YOUR WORD

"Let your yes be YES. Let your no be NO."
Matthew 5:37

One day Jesus was sitting with His followers and teaching them many important lessons. All the things He taught them were really about being brave. One lesson in particular was about doing what you say you're going to do. Jesus wants His children to be people who keep their word. People can rely and count on others who make promises and keep them. God is the great promise-keeper. The Bible is filled with His promises, and He has kept every one of them.

Jesus is building you up as a brave young boy by showing you how to live a life of integrity. For example, when you tell your parents that you will clean your room and you keep it clean, you live out this lesson. When you tell a friend that you will help him and you do, you are keeping your word.

God doesn't want His children just to say words that sound good to get their way. He wants you to be very simple in the life you live so you don't have to worry about saying things that aren't true.

JESUS, HELP ME TO AVOID SAYING THINGS THAT AREN'T TRUE. HELP ME TO KEEP MY PROMISES SO THAT MY CHARACTER WILL REMAIN ONE OF INTEGRITY.

DO NOT JUDGE

*"Do not say what is wrong in other people's lives.
Then other people will not say what is wrong in your life."*
MATTHEW 7:1

Not judging others is a really big deal to God. Jesus is the Messiah, and He alone judges because He alone died to save people from their sins. Judging people puts them on the defensive and hurts feelings. This is not the way Jesus wants His followers to live. Realizing that everyone makes a lot of mistakes helps brave people stay humble before God in the way they live and treat others.

Sometimes people like to judge because it makes them feel better about themselves. They might not feel as much of a mistake-maker as the people they judge. But this is not what Jesus wants. Having brave faith means trusting that at the cross everyone is equal!

Spend time thinking about all the ways you might judge somebody—by the way they dress, by the way they talk, by the way they do things. Instead of judging others, Jesus wants you to use that energy to see the mistakes you make and come to Him for forgiveness.

GOD, PLEASE HELP ME TO SEE OTHERS LIKE YOU SEE THEM.
HELP ME NOT TO JUDGE OTHERS. I WANT TO HELP AND NOT HURT.
I WANT TO UPLIFT PEOPLE AND NOT TEAR THEM DOWN.

GOD'S FISHERMEN

"Do not be afraid. From now on you will fish for men."
LUKE 5:10

Jesus had a friend named Peter. You might be familiar with his story. Peter was a fisherman and a hard worker who was also strong and brave. He knew how to get a job done. When Peter first met Jesus, he saw a miracle take place that helped him want to quit his job and follow Jesus.

Jesus had asked to borrow Peter's fishing boat so He could teach a crowd who had gathered. When Jesus was done preaching, He told Peter to take the boat out to deeper water so he and his friends could catch some fish. Peter was discouraged. He told Jesus that they had fished all night and caught nothing. Still, Peter obeyed, saying that he wanted to do what Jesus told him to do.

The Bible says that the fishermen caught so many fish, the nets started to break! When Peter saw what was happening, He told Jesus to get away from him because he was a sinner. Jesus told him not to be afraid and that from that time on, Peter and his friends would fish for people.

LORD, I WANT TO BE BRAVE LIKE PETER AND PUT ALL MY HOPE IN YOU. EVEN WHEN I DON'T UNDERSTAND, HELP ME TO REMEMBER HOW POWERFUL YOU ARE!

GO TO JESUS

"For God so loved the world that He gave His only Son. Whoever puts his trust in God's Son will not be lost but will have life that lasts forever."

JOHN 3:16

Jesus wants you to be brave and follow Him just like His disciples did! Study your Bible so you will be equipped with the truth. That's what one man named Nicodemus did. Nicodemus was a very powerful man in terms of his position as a leader of the Jewish people. The Bible says he was a proud keeper of the law. Despite his pride, Nicodemus knew that Jesus was very special. He went to Him at night and said he knew that Jesus must have come from God.

Jesus told Nicodemus that he had to be born again of water and of the Spirit of God. Nicodemus was confused at first, so Jesus explained what He meant (see John 3:1–21). Jesus said that God loved the world so much He sent His only Son to save it. All who put their trust in Jesus will be saved.

Think about what must have been going through the man's mind as he stood there listening to Jesus. Nicodemus was obviously moved, because later on he told his friends that they needed to be careful when they judged others. Finally, Nicodemus helped a man named Joseph prepare the Lord's body for burial after His crucifixion. Nicodemus learned how to be brave for God!

JESUS, HELP ME TO HOPE IN ALL YOUR PROMISES.

GREAT VICTORIES

*Hezekiah trusted in the Lord, the God of
Israel. There was no one like him.*
2 KINGS 18:5

God has great plans for you. Keep trusting Him. A brave king named Hezekiah did this very thing. Back in the days of kings, a lot of them were not very nice. They liked to do whatever they wanted, but Hezekiah trusted God and had a close relationship with Him. Hezekiah was brave and faithful to God because he understood that God was always with him.

Hezekiah's own father, Ahaz, was a wicked king. When it was Hezekiah's turn to take over, the first thing he did was clean up the castle. He got rid of all the pagan altars and idols. He reopened the temple in Jerusalem so the people could worship God the right way. Hezekiah wanted to make sure that everybody's eyes were turned back to the one true God. The Bible says that because of Hezekiah's faithfulness, God blessed him and made him prosper in whatever he set out to do.

Think about the things in your life that point people to God. Do what it takes to change your habits if some things in your life don't bring God honor. That's really brave living!

LORD, HEZEKIAH DID WHATEVER IT TOOK TO ACHIEVE GREAT
VICTORY IN YOUR NAME. HELP ME TO DO THE SAME.

FAITHFUL OBEDIENCE

He keeps safe the souls of His faithful ones.
PSALM 97:10

People are watching how you act. They will quickly see that you are different in a great way. They will wonder what makes you different, and that will give you an opportunity to tell them about Jesus and how He has transformed your life. That's what a woman named Rahab did.

Rahab lived in a big city called Jericho. A lot of people lived there, and they didn't love God. Rahab was an outcast because she had made a lot of bad choices. But God is so awesome that He decided to touch Rahab's heart and save her.

Rahab went on to help God's people destroy the city. You remember the story about the walls of Jericho falling when the Israelites marched around the city seven times. Everyone lost their lives except Rahab and her family. Rahab didn't worry about people's comments. She was only concerned about what God wanted. By being obedient, Rahab brought God's salvation to her house. By God's grace, she was saved and given a second chance.

LORD, HELP ME TO BE AWARE THAT PEOPLE ARE WATCHING HOW I RESPOND TO THINGS IN LIFE. HELP ME TO OVERCOME MY BAD DECISIONS BY TRUSTING IN YOUR FAITHFULNESS.

OVERCOMER

But the Lord knows how to help men who are
right with God when they are tempted.
2 PETER 2:9

At times you will be tempted to do the wrong thing or not do the right thing. Either way, being brave means staying right with God through prayer and asking Him to forgive you when you mess up. God will always take care of you. Being brave means you have a plan for handling stressful situations.

As you grow, choosing friends who are kind and positive is very important. If you are always hanging around people who make the wrong choices, their bad behavior will rub off on you. No one is perfect, but deciding that what God wants is the most important thing in your life will help you overcome challenges.

Starting each day by having a quiet time with God will help you keep your priorities straight. When a situation comes up, think about how God would want you to handle yourself. Be brave and do the right thing. God is proud of you.

LORD, THANK YOU FOR HELPING ME ALL THE TIME. I DON'T WANT TO TAKE YOU FOR GRANTED. I DON'T WANT TO GET SO COMFORTABLE THAT I GET LAZY WHEN IT COMES TO MY QUIET TIMES WITH YOU. LET ME ALWAYS WANT TO STAND UP FOR WHAT'S RIGHT AND BRING YOU GLORY!

SPIRIT OF POWER

For God did not give us a spirit of fear. He gave us a spirit of power and of love and of a good mind.
2 TIMOTHY 1:7

Gain courage daily from God's Word. Have faith that God will always be faithful to give you everything you need to complete the tasks He gives you. All throughout the Bible, you will read that God does not want His children to be afraid. In fact, the scriptures say that He has given His people a spirit of power, of love, and of a good mind. With Jesus on your side, you are a powerful young man who is training to do mighty things for God's kingdom. The enemy wants you to be okay with laziness and selfish pride because he knows what you can achieve otherwise.

God has also given you a spirit of love. This will help you treat others the way Jesus treats you! Doing everything in love means that you are obeying the Lord's command of treating others the way you want to be treated. Care for others in love the way Jesus cares for you.

Finally, God has given you a spirit of a good mind so that you will be able to know the right thing to do in any situation. Remembering all these gifts will help you be brave and courageous no matter what!

GOD, THANK YOU FOR BLESSING ME. PLEASE HELP ME TO FOCUS ON THE GIFTS YOU'VE GIVEN ME. HELP ME TO BE MORE LIKE JESUS EACH DAY.

BEGINNING AND END

"I am the First and the Last. I am the beginning and the end. To anyone who is thirsty, I will give the water of life. It is a free gift."

REVELATION 21:6

Jesus has been given many names, but one of them is very powerful to remember on your journey of being brave. That name is Alpha and Omega. Those are the first and last letters of the Greek alphabet and are a fitting title for Jesus. He is the first and the last—the beginning and end of everything.

When you think about being brave, put Jesus first. Before you do anything, ask Jesus for direction. Putting Him first will make everything make sense. Jesus was present in the beginning before the earth was formed. He's with you now, ready to go first. So start your day by praying when you get up in the morning. Ask Jesus to go before you in everything you do.

When Jesus is also last, you end your day in prayer, thanking Him for all of His blessings and lifting up words of praise. You are never alone, for Jesus is always with you. He is the Alpha who goes before you and the Omega who protects you from behind. Nothing can keep you from being brave when you live life this way.

DEAR JESUS, THANK YOU FOR MAKING ME BRAVE. HELP ME TO LIVE MY LIFE IN A WAY THAT WILL MAKE YOU KNOWN TO AS MANY PEOPLE AS POSSIBLE. IN YOUR MIGHTY NAME I PRAY. AMEN!

SCRIPTURE INDEX

OLD TESTAMENT

NEW TESTAMENT

MORE ENCOURAGEMENT AND WISDOM FOR BRAVE BOYS LIKE YOU!

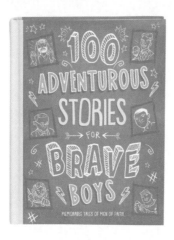

100 Adventurous Stories for Brave Boys

Boys are history-makers! And this deeply compelling storybook proves it! This collection of 100 adventurous stories of Christian men—from the Bible, history, and today—will empower you to know and understand how men of great character have made an impact in the world and how much smaller our faith (and the biblical record) would be without them.

Hardback / 978-1-64352-356-9